PRAISE FOR MIKE FALOON

"Mike Faloon is the kind of writer, both in fiction and in cultural criticism, who makes you believe in the short but powerful piece all over again. His characters are the kinds of people Sherwood Andersen or James Thurber would have written about; ordinary people trapped in trying, but ordinary lives and usually able to laugh at their circumstances. Faloon consistently and often hilariously points out the little idiosyncrasies that make life worth living and he has an unusually sharp lens for human foibles, but also realizing the hidden strength of fictional characters, real-life sports has-beens, or challenging hard-to-characterize squonk jazz musicians. He's been one of my favorite writers for a long time in both fiction and non-fiction prose, because as a writer, Faloon actually roots for whoever he is writing about."

–**Brian Cogan**, *Everything I Ever Needed to Know About _____ I Learned From Monty Python*

"I'd rather read Faloon's musings on jazz and baseball, than listen to or watch either. That is because he isn't really writing about baseball or jazz, but of larger human endeavors, of connections and miscues, of deeds and dreams. And like his short story collection *The Hanging Gardens of Split Rock*, the essays in *The Other Night at Quinn's* are immediately engaging, while also embedding themselves for continued consideration. Faloon tells stories, but he is also a master of the slow reveal."

–**Kevin Dunn**, *Global Punk*

"Any good player knows jazz is about listening. With the deftness of the musicians he writes about, Mike Faloon shows his inimitable writing and listening skills, making sophisticated connections on the fly and shaping them, afterwards, into essays which resonate even if you don't know the music."

–**Michael T. Fournier**, *Swing State*

ALSO BY MIKE FALOON

The Other Night at Quinn's

New Adventures in the Sonic Underground

The Other Night at Quinn's

New Adventures in the Sonic Underground
By Mike Faloon

RAZORCAKE / GORSKY PRESS
LOS ANGELES, CALIFORNIA
2017

RZC/GP

Razorcake / Gorsky Press
PO Box 42129
Los Angeles, CA 90042
razorcake.org
gorskypress.com

Cover photos by Michael Bogdanffy-Kriegh
Book and cover design by Todd Taylor

For Maggie & Sean

FOREWORD

SOMETHING

Music is a love beast
A sky dragon
A snake
A humming bird
A crocodile
If you put
Your ear close
You can hear
Something

Walking into Quinn's for the first time was a bit like walking into a Norman Rockwell illustration viewed through the lens of *The Twilight Zone*. "Are you kidding me?" was my first condescending thought. I live just up the road a piece where I virtually never play, at least not the kind of music I get to play in Europe, or Chicago, or New York, or Seattle. Now I'm in Beacon, New York, in what appears to be a luncheonette, about to play what? Okay, it was a nice idea. I know Beacon and I grew up in this area. How long would it take to get thrown out? I remember being asked in Poughkeepsie where I live, "People actually pay you to play that shit?"

So much for my prejudice and blatant stupidity. It didn't take long to be caught up in the warmth and hospitality that is Quinn's. James Keepnews and Steve Ventura set the mood and you would believe you had been transported to *Cheers*, where everybody knows your name. I began to imagine what it might have been like to walk into The Five Spot and coming upon Ornette Coleman or Monk and Trane, so much exciting, challenging music time after time. So many enthusiastic supporters, risk takers ready to jump into the deep end of the pool. People like Mike Faloon, always sitting at the lunch counter, curiously making notes with a gleam in his eye and a smile on his face listening to something, listening to everything.

Once I thought, Why not call Quinn's The New Five Spot on the Hudson? Nah! Quinn's is just fine, thank you. Mike has captured the spirit of those Monday nights and shares the energy, warmth, and deeply personal experiences in a way that puts the reader in a seat at the lunch counter. From a personal perspective, his words conjure a treasure trove of bittersweet memories.

The chapter titled "A Midwinter's Dream" particularly touched me, as Dominic Duval sadly passed away in 2016. We had been together with Trio X for eighteen wonderful years. In 1999 we recorded a duo performance called *The Dream Book* and on that Monday night at Quinn's we came as close to a reprise as we ever had.

One frequent visitor to those Monday nights was my longtime friend Jerry Starpoli. Jerry had an aversion to cold weather but he was there for the duo with Dominic. He complained bitterly about some of the loud-talking patrons, but he loved the magic of the music and he would have loved this book. *The Other Night at Quinn's* is an amazing journey of love.

–Joe McPhee

Dedicated to Craig Johnson

TABLE OF CONTENTS

Matt Dearborn at the sound board | Michael Bogdanffy-Kriegh

James Keepnews, Joe McPhee, and Michael Wimberly | Michael Bogdanffy-Kriegh

INTRODUCTION

Ever since the sensory overload of my first enormo-dome concert, squinting into the distance as the Police slammed into the chorus of "Roxanne" and thousands stood deafened by the roar and blinded by the floodlights, I've craved the buzz of live music. Tracking down, anticipating, meeting up, savoring, remembering, retelling, all of it. Later I discovered the intimacy of house and club shows, leaning against a cramped stage as dozens cradled plastic cups of cheap beer and howled along with Big Dipper charging through "She's Fetching."

I told myself that I moved to New York City to find a job but access to shows was the greater motivation. After years of living in Queens, my wife and I relocated upstate. I looked for live music close to our new home but the local listings were few and clogged with cover bands. I still ventured into the city, but often had to leave shows early to catch the last train upstate only to slump home at three in the morning. I assumed over time the missed encores and bleary-eyed mornings would diminish live music's appeal.

* * *

Kumiko, the Treasure Hunter opens with the title character clutching a treasure map, walking along a beach in Japan. She enters a small cave and digs up a VHS copy of the Coen Brothers' *Fargo*. Kumiko becomes infatuated with the film. Other than sleepwalking through her job and shrugging off phone calls from her mother, she does nothing other than watch the movie, her face aglow as she sits on the floor of her dark apartment inches from the screen, losing herself in the search for the next treasure's clues.

* * *

Living in New York led me to new substreams of the DIY underground, the countless people making music, movies, zines, comics, and books. They placed creativity over commerce. By the time I moved upstate, though, my default preferences were still set to underground pop and punk, melody and brevity and songwriting above all else. Lengthy improvisations rarely, if ever, entered the equation.

Then I stumbled across a live music series at Quinn's in nearby Beacon. Quinn's offered a provocative, though seemingly antithetical, mix of improvised and experimental music. I was overwhelmed by the performances, lost in the best way. I found myself writing in response, leaving shows with sheets of frantically scrawled notes, posting columns online, trying to puzzle things out and orient myself.

* * *

Kumiko becomes particularly obsessed with the scene in which Steve Buscemi's character Carl Showalter frantically scrapes through layers of snow to bury a suitcase full of ransom money. She also takes at face value *Fargo*'s prologue, "This is a true story." Kumiko believes the riches are actually buried in Northern Minnesota waiting for her to discover.

Despite having little money, speaking less English, and knowing no one along the way, she plunges into a journey from Japan to Minnesota.

* * *

Before there was Beacon, there were Fishkill Landing and Matteawan, neighboring villages with distinctly different personalities situated about sixty miles north of New York City. The former was a transportation hub along the Hudson River. The latter was a factory town which drew its power from Fishkill Creek. They sat alongside each other, unofficially sharing an extended Main Street, a river-to-creek stretch of nearly two miles.

* * *

To prepare for her adventure, Kumiko makes a map based on *Fargo*. She pauses the movie, counts footsteps and fence posts, tapes sheets of paper to the screen and traces images, sketches approximations in her notebook. Then she sews a treasure map with a bright red "x" to mark the spot. She uses the map to guide herself and communicate with the people she encounters. She needs to orient herself and wants other people to see things as she does, share her perspective. She's developed her own language and grammar to navigate the world.

* * *

George Saunders: "As I've gotten older my view of the world has shifted. I find life so beautiful and also so hard to pin down. For me the process of sitting down to write a story is to keep your eyes open all the time, to keep yourself mystified. You go out in the world, see what it is. It's just as fresh as it was when you were eighteen. Go out there and experience it, come back in befuddled."

* * *

The shows at Quinn's left me mystified and challenged my navigation skills. The farther the musicians ventured, the more my thoughts drifted. Over time I found myself steering into those reactions. The wanderings found their way into my notes, enhanced more than detracted, background to foreground, distraction to essence.

* * *

Fishkill Landing and Matteawan merged in 1913 to form the city of Beacon. The last part of the city to develop was near the intersection of Chestnut and Main streets. It was difficult building in this part of town, which lay on the western outskirts of the former Fishkill Landing and the eastern edge of Matteawan. A small underground stream periodically yielded quicksand-like conditions, and the area was prone to flooding.

Quinn's is located just past that intersection, just past the seam where the two towns came together, just above those underground currents. Though an unlikely place for things to take root, it's become a setting in which disparate forces merge. *The Other Night at Quinn's* represents the maps I made to guide myself along the way.

Joe McPhee | Michael Bogdanffy-Kriegh

A Midwinter's Dream
Joe McPhee & Dominic Duval

*"One of these days we're going to get into it
Way on over our heads"*
—Camper Van Beethoven, "One of These Days"

"Going out to see free jazz, that's risky behavior."

I'm sitting at a luncheonette counter, elbows on Formica, Tiffany lights overhead, confused by an incongruous set of factors. Improvised music at an upstate diner on a snowy Monday night in January. Like the quote above, overheard in a conversation between the diner's owner and a friend, it's a dicey proposition.

I'm here to see Joe McPhee. I first read about him in a review which likened his 1971 album, *Nation Time*, to Herbie Hancock's *Head Hunters*. Their Venn diagrams overlap but *Nation Time* hits harder and travels further afield. It's an exhilarating album, easy to enjoy yet elusive and difficult to classify. The emotions overflow and the instruments pin the meters fueling songs that are long and melodic, unhinged and hypnotic.

Moments after reading about *Nation Time* I was online looking for the vinyl, eventually settling for a download. Within a month, wanting an artifact and doubtful of digital technology's durability, I tracked down the CD and eventually the LP, too. I never buy releases in multiple formats but I wanted to experience the infinite mysteries of *Nation Time* in every variation.

I assumed seeing McPhee live would require reservations at a Manhattan club, a too expensive cover for a too small table, or having to decipher cryptic directions to a loft in the depths of Brooklyn. But now McPhee, over four decades into his career and just back from another European tour, is right over there, at the end of the counter, sipping a draft and talking with friends with the informal air of my uncle's Saturday morning breakfast club.

Quinn's has that informal air, too. Built in the early fifties, it retains the look and feel of a vintage diner. The white counter wobbles, the seats swivel, and the pie case's sliding glass doors are coated with condensation. The layout is long and narrow, like CBGB, with people shuffling by stage right as they pass through the front door. I'd walked past Quinn's before but never come in. They were closed, between owners. I was drawn to the sign, the one that hangs over the sidewalk, the one with the missing "n." I crossed the street and stood outside looking in, unable to make out much in the murkiness. I figured it was the kind of place that served the best food in town or couldn't pass a health inspection. Perhaps both. I asked my wife what she'd heard about Quinn's. She works in Beacon, knows the town better. She'd heard about the ownership change and that a lot of locals missed the diner but nothing about live music.

McPhee is joined by bassist Dominic Duval. Their sets loosely revolve around *The Dream Book*, their 1999 tribute to Ornette Coleman.

"Playing around some of his tunes," as McPhee puts it. "Around" rather than "around with." The choice of prepositions sticks in my head for days. McPhee doesn't talk much from stage, but he's adept at providing a frame of reference. "We borrow from the literature," he says, "and we add to the continuum. I don't think Bach or Beethoven would like to hear their music the way it's usually played. They'd want it to carry on." He also recognizes the chances he and Duval are taking (and us, too, by extension). "Thank you for your indulgence because we can make a big mess of it."

Dominic Duval pursues his own tangents but is just as likely to repeat phrases, double back to melodic ideas. For most of the first set McPhee and Duval are subtle and subdued, conversational. But then McPhee rips through, reaches for the high end of his register and beyond, blows a blustery cloud of atonality. His subsequent plummet is just as sudden. He's punctured something in the room. Most of the crowd is with him, applauding and exchanging "Check *that* out" looks.

For some he's crossed the line between risk and reward. A few heads turn with sour looks of "What the...?" A couple of conversations break out, rise above the music. The table behind me has been talking in hushed tones. Now they're too loud, disruptive, emboldened—*Things got weird, we've given ourselves license to blather.* I expect to see twenty-somethings when I turn around. Instead they're white hairs, one and all. Generation Glowbox may have a sick addiction to their devices but the Millennials up front maintain eyeballs on bandstand.

McPhee opens the second set beating the tar out of a white plastic saxophone. "Sometimes it stays in tune," he says. The sight alone— a player of such renown playing an instrument of such cheap construction—is like watching Henry Aaron swat away with a Wiffle bat, using that sweet swing in such a way that you wonder why he'd ever use a wood bat.

By night's end I'm still experiencing some residual disbelief but free jazz in a diner is making more sense. At the end of the show the M.C. announces the sessions will continue every Monday this month and next, with more to follow, he says, if the series is extended. This could become a habit.

Mike Dopazo | Michael Bogdanffy-Kriegh

Beginning to See the Light
Mike Dopazo Trio

"At the peak of my February darkness
I knew I had to find a great escape"
—Jack Grace, "Morning Margaritas"

Main Street is quiet. Salt crunches underfoot. Gas station banners flap in the breeze. I stuff my hands in my coat pockets and walk faster, watching my breath hang in the cold night air. Inside it's crowded but I'm able to get a seat at the counter, which has me feeling a bit jittery, self-conscious. I'm not sure how long I'll be staying. I want to see myself as a John McNulty type, listening, blending in, but how do the regulars see me, and am I tipping enough for someone who's taking a good seat but doesn't drink much?

Joining saxophonist Mike Dopazo are bassist Scott Fragala and drummer Jon Doty. Dopazo is confident and plays with a bright, assertive sound, expressive and tuneful. He credits the legends whose songs they're interpreting: Sonny Rollins, Billy Strayhorn, Wayne Shorter. It's no surprise I take to their set.

When my friend Brendan read my previous piece he said that I should turn around more, include more atmospheric details to fill out the setting. It's good advice. I intend to heed it, but I don't, not yet. Presently I'm distracted by the quote posted next to the cash register:

> "The have and have nots
> are bleeding in the tub
> That's New York's future
> not mine"
> 3/2/42 – 10/27/13

I don't recognize the lyrics but the second line reminds me of *The Godfather*, Frankie Five Angels' bathtub suicide. I don't want the image to stick. The band bails me out. So do the conversations I hear. Over my right shoulder: "You ever go hop hunting? I've heard there's wild hops growing in the park." Over my left: "They have Genny Cream Ale!" It isn't the choice itself that catches my attention. Genny Cream Ale is cheap swill. It's the tone of voice, the gleeful, cheap beer joy; "You *have* that?!" Maybe I'm magnifying a minor detail. Dopazo and company have me in a good mood and sitting among the flannel and tattoos, the bearded and the weird, I trust, perhaps more than I should or need to, that I'm among my kind of people.

I never would have guessed that part of my February escape would entail going to a diner on a Monday night in Beacon. It's rare we have access to things of this nature upstate. We day trip into New York City, dip into its culture, but the city is a region away and I'd rather support something local.

I read the quote behind the bar again. I still can't place it. I ask the bartender. "They're from a Lou Reed song," he responds. That's when I notice the dates beneath the quote. The band carries on, conjuring Dean Moriarty's *On the Road* monologue about a bandleader who clearly knows "it." Dopazo and company hit full stride with a Thelonious Monk tune, pushing the tempo just right, then mix in an original, "One, Two."

Dopazo announces they're going to play one more before taking a break. That's when I abandon my plan to leave early. It comes down to a look from Dopazo. Preparing for the next tune, he scans the room and a look flashes across his face. It intimates he isn't finding what he seeks, maybe something we aren't providing, at least in that moment. Or maybe it's not a response to something external, perhaps it's something within. Either way it doesn't anger him, doesn't wilt him. It spurs him on. I think of the crummy, often disheartening, ratios that so many creative people endure. The hours of practice and heartache, travel and trial and error that outnumber, often outweigh, the moments of satisfaction. Maybe I misread the glare, but it's why I stay.

Cooper-Moore | Michael Bogdanffy-Kriegh

Tunes and Tales in Equal Measure
Cooper-Moore & Patrick Brennan

"You all didn't come here to hear stories. You came to hear music."
Cooper-Moore proposes getting back to songs.

Someone calls out, "It's *all* music."

Moore grins. This is an audience he can work with.

Outside it is another miserable night. The snow banks inch ever higher.
The icy street corners grow more perilous. I was visiting family in
Syracuse over the weekend. I went looking for driveway salt because
I've been unable to find any down this way. When I finally tracked down
a supply I was told it was the last stash in town and there was a strict
one-bag per customer policy. What kind of long, lousy winter are we
experiencing when Syracuse—literally nicknamed the Salt City—is
running out of salt?

Brennan opens the night blazing away on his alto sax. His sound isn't easy to file. It's not totally free, unhinged, but what it's tethered to is hard to say. It's not exactly melodic either. His sound is puzzling and inviting. He could hold an audience unaccompanied, but he's joined by another performer who can hold an audience on his own, Cooper-Moore, the madcap maker and player of instruments that are at once familiar and unusual.

Presently Moore has a two-part drum in his lap—a bass drum head and a snare drum head. In his right hand a stick and a mallet. In his left hand a brush. I can barely figure out how he balances everything yet alone operates them. One moment he's using sticks on the heads, pushing out a syncopated funk. The next he turns the snare head on its side and presses it against the bass drum head, which sounds like a stand-up bass. He's a terrific complement to Brennan and his equally hard-to-pin down sound; their sounds melt together. I wish I could throw some of that on my driveway.

Off-stage Moore is a globe-trotting educator. He's led teacher workshops in Tupelo, Mississippi, helped kids in Mexico City write an opera, and worked with teen rappers in the suburbs of Paris. Or maybe it was rap in Mexico and opera in France. The details come fast and furious and I can't catch everything. Likewise when he describes the numerous handmade instruments he plays throughout the show. His fretless banjo has a circular body cut from a closet door. The exterior is paper mâché colored with instant coffee grounds and sealed with floor wax. The diddley bow, a single string strung along a board five or six feet long, can be plucked or bowed or played with sticks—bass and drum in one. The diddley bow hails from the rural south, "regarded as a kids' instrument," says Moore, "it was first mentioned by Pythagoras…. It's all about the one."

Moore built his handmade harp when he was living in Virginia in the mid-'70s. He took a trip to D.C. and saw a Brazilian man playing a Paraguayan harp. Moore looked into buying one for himself only to find it cost $8,000. A short while later, when he was at home gardening, Moore broke a hoe and placed the broken handle by his bedside. "Hoe handle, hoe handle, what will you be?" he called out. Four hours of labor and eight bucks later he'd fashioned the "horizontal hoe handle harp," complete with fishing line strings.

I posted the write-up about my first trip to Quinn's online. The feedback was surprising, more responses than recent music reviews I've posted, mostly people from Beacon as far as I can tell, none of whom are familiar. One of them is James Keepnews, the M.C. and curator of these shows. "On my honor," he writes, "all of February's Mondays are going to be incredible and notably distinct from one another. Please make the introductions when you're there." I introduce myself and he graciously answers my many questions about the shows, tonight's, previous, and upcoming.

Looking across the room, past the stage, and through the windows streaked with condensation, I see snow. It reminds me of Cicely, Alaska, the small town from the old CBS series *Northern Exposure*. Despite living in remote Alaska the cast somehow found itself interacting with out-of-towners of all stripes each week. (My favorite being Ed Chigliak's ongoing correspondence with the likes of Martin Scorsese and Woody Allen.) Beacon is hardly Alaska—recent appearances to the contrary—but I'm still struck by the small-town-to-big-talent ratio.

The crowd is slower to assemble tonight—probably due to the weather—but no less enthralled. One of my favorite sights, just before the end of the first set, is the row of motionless heads at the counter, everyone transfixed by a mix of *That sounds so cool* and *How are they doing that?* The applause breaks are tempered a bit, but I attribute that to momentary collective confusion, not sure whether the latest blitz of beautiful madness is pausing or ending. And Moore keeps telling stories.

"I ain't afraid of dead people, I just don't want to look at them. I'm not afraid of death or dying, but it doesn't suit me to be looking at it." Moore goes on to describe the time a friend's elderly father was sent home from hospice. Moore called to ask about visiting on the weekend, but his wife said he shouldn't wait. When he called back he learned that the father had just died. Moore said he'd be right over. Upon arriving at the friend's apartment his senses were overloaded by the sight of the father propped up in bed, the smell of pot, and the sounds of John and Alice Coltrane's *Cosmic Music*. A father's final wishes granted.

James announces that the Monday night series has been continued through next month. Meanwhile, Brennan and Moore hold court after the show, sharing stories as they break down and pack up, twirling wing nuts and clasping cases as people pass into the night.

Schoonmakers, near Main Street & North Chestnut | **Beacon Historical Society**

Midtown Market | **Beacon Historical Society**

Bev Turcy, Joe Turcy, & Betty Ann Coughlin

(Note: Quinn's is located at 330 Main Street. The building was constructed in 1951. Originally the space was occupied by a restaurant, George's, owned by the Charkalis family. Rose Quinn purchased the building in the early 1980s. She owned and operated the original Quinn's until selling to the current owners in 2013.

While researching the building's history, I met Bev Turcy at the Beacon City Building Department. A lifelong resident of Beacon, she shared memories of George's and Quinn's as she walked me through the list of previous owners. Later, we met up along with her husband Joe and sister Betty Ann.)

Joe: George's Restaurant was a hangout for kids back in the day.

Bev: It was owned by Charkalis but we called it George's.

Betty Ann: I went to school with [the owner's] son.

Bev: He owned it in '51. It was not a restaurant-restaurant, more of a sandwich shop.

Betty Ann: A soda fountain-type thing.

Bev: And the kids just started congregating there.

Joe: We all hung out in the back after school.

Bev: It was a place where everybody went to be together. A mass of kids walking from Beacon High School to George's after school, or from the field to George's after a football game.

Joe: At one time there were three sections here. The Mountain Boys, the Swamp Angels, then down by the river was the River Rats. Back in those days you didn't cross lines. My mother would say, Don't go across the crick, don't go across the crick. We lived in the swamp area. She [Bev] lived right on the edge of the River Rats.

Betty Ann: When we were kids, it was nice here.

Bev: Oh yeah. We had, what, five drug stores?

Joe: We had Grant's across the street.

Bev: We had Schoonmakers. Fishman's. Shuman's Army-Navy where everyone went for their jeans and sneakers. Before you were old enough to hang out in George's, every single person you knew was on Main Street Friday night for the open stores.

Joe: And we had a lot of men's shops. We had Wright Brothers Clothing and suits and stuff. My father bought me a suit there when I first went to high school.

Bev: Shuman's Army-Navy sold a lot more than just jeans and sneakers. It sold clothes. When my mother died my son was a teenager; all he had was jeans and sneakers. I said to my daughter, "Take him down to Shuman's and get him two sets of clothes." I gave her a signed, blank check. The only store in the world I would ever, ever give a blank check to. You could do that with Shuman's.

Joe: In Shuman's Army-Navy store she had a nice women's shop.

Bev: I used to buy all my clothes from her.

Joe: Christmas time, boom, down there I go. And she [the owner/manager] knew Bev's size and everything, I had no problems.

Betty Ann: What was the shoe store that used to X-ray your feet? You used to step in this little X-ray machine. That must have been real good for us, right? Every time you get a pair of shoes you get your feet X-rayed for size.

Bev: That might have been Florsheim shoes. We called it an X-ray. But technically I think it was another type of technology. It was a machine you looked into and saw your feet, including the bones. Your size was determined by this.

* * *

Bev: And when it turned into Quinn's, they had the best food.

Joe: Homemade breads.

Bev: Homemade breads, homemade soups.

Betty Ann: Her [owner Rose Quinn] food was excellent. She had a place on the other end of town for years. The Alps. She cooked there.

Joe: Where the empty lot is. That's where Quinn's originally was but it was a little hole-in-the-wall. She had a little restaurant here that was four or five stools at the counter and maybe three booths and that was it. Then she moved into George's Restaurant. In the '80s, Bev?

Bev: '85. She only did breakfast and lunch.

Joe: I used to go over to Quinn's all the time.

Bev: Everybody did. In the morning it was the place all the businessmen met.

Betty Ann: All the doctors and lawyers.

Joe: I went in for the homemade bread. Toasted homemade bread and coffee, I was happy.

Betty Ann: She made the best pies.

Bev: Good soups.

Betty Ann: She had a special every day. She was there very early in the morning to make bread. Unbelievable. She worked like crazy. And when she was married her husband did nothing. He talked to everybody. That's all he ever did.

Joe: Nothing.

Bev: He talked. Collected money and talked.

Betty Ann: That is exactly what he did. It was horrible when they closed.

* * *

Joe: The city of Beacon was pretty rough back in the '80s. Things were going downhill.

Bev: It wasn't a place where you hung out on Main Street.

Joe: It was crazy around here, boy.

Betty Ann: Nothing but boarded up buildings.

Bev: It wasn't until Dia[1] came. Dia was the start of it all.

Betty Ann: And I can't figure out why because that is the dumbest...

Bev: Well, that might be you but there are a lot of people that are into it.

Betty Ann: I don't understand it.

Bev: And once Dia came, it was slow for a while then all of a sudden...

Joe: Boom.

Bev: Something happened.

---

1 Dia:Beacon is a contemporary art museum opened in 2003.

Ted Daniel | Michael Bogdanffy-Kriegh

In Search of
Jay Rosen, Ted Daniel, & Michael Marcus

"My future crept up on me much like a heart attack
The straight life is calling me and I ain't calling back"
—The Ergs!, "On the Interstate"

I've heard Dasono described as a Los Angeles book gang.

* * *

School wiped me out today, unusually so, left me dragging in ways I hadn't felt since my first year. I felt a lack of clarity, a haze, a midday malaise. My science lesson tumbleweeded. (*Bueller? Bueller?*) I hit all the marks in my lesson plan and the kids completed their tasks, but something was off. I regrouped during my prep period thinking of tonight's show, eager to see drummer Jay Rosen. He's in Trio X with Joe McPhee and Dominic Duval. When they played a few weeks back I overheard McPhee say, "We need to get Jay up here."

* * *

Last summer I was in Los Angeles for a couple of readings, staying with my friend Todd. We've toured together numerous times over the years. We know each other pretty well. But one night at a house show Todd wore an out-of-character sleeveless jean jacket with a pink skull patch that read Dasono. Three other people wore matching sleeveless jean jackets with identical patches but no one commented on them.

* * *

The rest of tonight's line up is intriguing, too. Ted Daniel and Michael Marcus, trumpet and clarinet. A brass and a reed trading ideas, overlapping dialogue, like *Glengarry Glen Ross*. Marcus plants his feet and twists his torso, movement along the x-axis. Daniel moves along the y. One moment he's bent over, blasting at the stage. The next he bends back, a reflex angle flaring upward. Like an ordered pair, you need both variables to coordinate yourself. Rosen glues them together, left hand on snare, right working the rhythm.

I arrive just as a couple vacates prime turf at the counter. The bartender recognizes me and introduces himself as Mark. I order and turn to face the perfect sight line; I can see all three musicians without having to shift. To my left a middle-aged man looks into his soup bowl and nods along. He sees my notebook and introduces himself. David is from out of town, visiting a friend. He used to be a writer before "life got in the way." He likes what he's read from my online columns, except for a negative comment I made about Steely Dan's Donald Fagen. Compliments are appreciated, but being told you're full of it can lead to a better conversation.

* * *

Last weekend I was at a show at Flywheel in Western Massachusetts. I ran into Paul, whom I hadn't seen in years. He and his wife had moved from Detroit to Atlanta to Boston. Their greatest challenge along the way was locating the local flavor in each town, "finding the weird," as he put it; the people reaching beyond the multiplex, forever tracking down the local points of interest, the things that distinguish one town from the next.

Paul lights up when I mention Beacon. He's heard that it's like Northampton. In subsequent conversations that night there are comparisons to Portland and Brooklyn. I appreciate those cities but want to see Beacon as unique. Some nights are easier than others. Walking to the bathroom I pass three kids climbing over the back of a booth, clamoring for their parents' attention. The parents are oblivious, seated at a neighboring table, talking and laughing over a cheese platter and drinks. My reactions flash from judgment to envy to imagining the note they will send to school the next day: "Ulysses, Edith, and Yolk were unable to complete their homework last night due to inquiry-based cultural enrichment, dig?!"

* * *

Todd tells me that Dasono is "a social book club. When people ask what we're reading, the answer is always *1984*. We drink beer, go to the occasional baseball game, and have plans for mini golf."

* * *

It's a Monday. It's a diner. It's cold, again. Not an obvious set of factors for staging a successful music series but part of maintaining the weird underground is pushing past, through and/or around the obvious. Top-flight talent helps. Jay Rosen swings and pings while Ted Daniel and Michael Marcus exchange ideas out front. They don't talk much. They don't go into backstories. They play, in sync at the top, then off they go.

Compatible but divergent, a musical split screen, trading spotlight time, going back and forth between solos. They're even better when playing simultaneously, one sound packed with details, an extended tracking shot, the opening to *A Touch of Evil*, the camera floating above the border town street, so many scenic details to absorb. The joy is being able to choose, deciding where to focus, what to tune into, with the tension of an impending explosion.

* * *

I ask Todd how he first came across underground culture. He mentioned the Velvet Underground, *Fear and Loathing in Las Vegas*, and making mix tapes from KUNV. "I cherish that electrically charged uncertainty, that mental map making, that clawing away, because it scraped inside me, etched me. That near-constant attraction/repulsion changed my polarity. Little did I know at the time that I had begun construction of my own personal magnet of weird."

* * *

Rosen concludes a solo flowing back and forth between the toms and snare before Daniel and Marcus return. The counter crowd nods our approval but over my shoulder I hear someone clap. I assume the people seated past the kitchen are here more for the talk than the tunes. It's reassuring to be set straight.

Daniel breaks out a mute for the next number. Muted trumpet goes even better with clarinet. Plus, there's the sight of him manipulating that metal disc, the delightfully analog way of the whole thing. The dam bursts on the final number, the shortest piece of the night, as loud as it is fast. It's almost too much, like having to shield your eyes from the midday sun, and it's over too soon.

On my way out James introduces me to Jay Rosen, who's hunched over a bowl of chili. Even though he's wearing the same floral print shirt from the show, seeing him now—post-gig—is like seeing a ballplayer out of uniform, in his civilians. "Oh, hey, nice to meet you," he says. "Did you like the music?" He's been playing out for nearly twenty-five years, recorded dozens of records, and toured the world. Yet his curiosity seems genuine, none of the guarded cool I've long projected on to jazz musicians.

I'm awake and alert as I step onto Main Street, ready to try that science lesson again.

Fuel Consumption Way Too Fast
The Jaimie Branch Trio

"The crowds and their coolers so soon will be gone
And we'll have our beach back"
—The Kluggmen, "We'll Have Our Beach Back"

Arrive early at Quinn's and you'll see instruments waiting on stage and musicians mingling. Chances are they've already caught up with Craig. He knows everyone and their records, too, though you'd have to prompt him on those. He's humble about his encyclopedic knowledge. The seat next to Craig is open. I order a drink and ask how he's doing. "Had a late night and a busy week," he says. "One set then I'm gone."

* * *

The brim of Jaimie Branch's White Sox cap is turned up and to the side. The tail of her belt hangs loose. Her backpack yields a piece of sheet metal that she tosses on the stage. Her look is laid back but she attacks from note one, up and out and gone, each push of her trumpet's valves is like a flame to wick, explosions flashing. It's incendiary, the work of a sonic subversive whose placement of materials is strategic and timing precise, maximizing impact and transforming the terrain.

* * *

I was recently talking with Steve, one of the owners of Quinn's, about a Toronto band that had invited Joe McPhee to play. He said they'd been around since the mid-'60s and have maintained a routine of playing every Monday, but couldn't recall their name. Nor could anyone else. Craig returned from a cigarette break, overheard a detail and asked, "Are you talking about the Nihilist Spasm Band?"

It's not like Craig to say that he's leaving early. I ask if his week's been good busy or stressful busy. "Fifty-fifty," he says. He mentions a doctor's appointment. I've noticed he hasn't been using his cane lately and wonder how that ties in but don't want to pry.

* * *

Branch tugs on her T-shirt, wipes her mouth on the collar. Bassist Brandon Lopez and drummer Mike Pride solo around and elevate one another, intertwined, a double helix spiraling upward and blazing ahead. Then it's rhythm section role reversal. Lopez rubs and slaps the side of his bass while Pride pulls a bow along the edge of a cymbal.

* * *

Early in Lynda Barry's *Syllabus* she revisits a notebook from the late '70s. At the time she was trying to be more observant, more open to experiences, get past thinking "nothing happened." She didn't want to feel compelled to "agree with, understand, [or] like" what she experienced. She wanted to "*just see.*"

* * *

I see a band humming along, a catamaran on the open sea, sailing on one hull, precariously close to tipping over. Though they hardly resemble the sailboat set seen in catalogs, coifs glued in place, shirts tucked in, smiles ready for toothpaste ads. The trio is more whaling crew, rough and tumble, beards and tats, appearances secondary, at best, to their riveting combination of sonic discord and social cohesion. All hands on deck, a group of three charged with the work of a dozen, inviting and averting disaster. Roles less rigidly defined, more fluid.

* * *

The time between sets is longer. The crowd thins but Craig is still here. He'll be part of the post-show hang, too. For now, we talk about the Mets, another unturned double play and just-short comeback, and the record collection he's thinking of selling off. I ask if he's feeling better, perhaps caught a second wind. "Not really," he says, "but the music's too good and the band deserves better."

* * *

Jacqueline Woodson's *Brown Girl Dreaming* is a beautifully sprawling memoir. Navigating the course of her childhood, Woodson transports us through early '60s Ohio to South Carolina to Brooklyn. She examines the relationships that shaped her—growing up in her sister's shadow, figuring out her absent father, grappling with her grandmother's Christian Science faith—and charts the evolution of a persona as bold and self-assured as it is graceful and tender.

* * *

There is a recombination of elements in the second set, more room to stretch, to breathe. Branch extinguishes the Molotov cocktails in favor of candles, takes the street fight tableside. She tilts her head to the side and cleans the slate before propelling a series of delicate, prolonged notes that go right through me, opening new possibilities as to what can be heard and felt. There's a density that I've not experienced before, something redemptive, reassuring, bigger than me. It's like the first time I heard the Minutemen. A friend asked me to make a copy of his *3-Way Tie for Last* cassette. I didn't know anything about the band or underground punk. I assumed that I would set the tape-to-tape deck in motion, confirm my negative assumptions about punk rock, and leave the room. Instead I stayed, slack jawed, glued to the band's live wire crackle and squawk, my eyes opened to colors I'd never before seen.

I reach for my phone to record Branch's solo but fumble to get it out in time. I'm not sure how committed I am to the idea. I don't want to take my eyes off the band, the moment seems so fragile and intimate, and even then I realize these sounds won't be on my phone later. They can't be captured, not completely. Much of the appeal of live improvised music is seeing the means and the ends, witnessing all that occurs between the notes, the deliberations and decisions, the wincing and grimacing and reaching.

* * *

One day in church school Woodson is asked to write a skit about the resurrection. She takes to the task with great enthusiasm. She asks if she can stand up and move about the stage. She asks if she can work by herself and tries to enhance the assignment by adding ideas of her own. She wants to include horses and cows. She wants to know what happens to animals when they die. Her choices meet with continual resistance. *Sit down. Leave out the animals. Stop asking questions.* Her desire to explore and inquire, to assert herself, to make the experience more distinctive, more unique, is squelched at every turn.

* * *

Branch paces, circles the stage, listens to her bandmates, picks up the sheet metal-turned-mute. Like a pitcher changing arm angles, she alters her delivery—up and down, side to side, diagonally—as well as her proximity to the microphone. She drops her right arm to her side, reveals the "Toucan spaceship" tattoo on her left forearm. Her right arm has a dog plane. Snuffian ruffians, she calls them. So many variables at her disposal yet stamping each moment with her indelible sound.

* * *

Toward the end of the night, a handful of us remaining, James takes the counter seat between Craig and me, leans over and says, "This reminds me of these late night sets I'd see downtown. Two, three in the morning. Playing to ten people. It's out of time, you know, like it's ours. You hold it closer."

Joe McPhee | Michael Bogdanffy-Kriegh

Joe McPhee, musician

I was an absolutely caught-up Miles Davis fan and I bought everything I could get my hands on. I had a copy of *Bags' Groove*, which I absolutely loved. I went to visit a friend who played a copy of Charles Mingus's *Pithecanthropus Erectus.* That opened my eyes completely, turned me around. I traded my *Bags' Groove* for *Pithecanthropus Erectus.*

Then I heard *Change of the Century* [Ornette Coleman], and I don't remember the title of the Eric Dolphy one, but it's the one with the kind of Salvador Dali-looking cover [*Out There*]. Wow. That was my entry into this other music.

I had been reading about Ornette Coleman and Eric Dolphy in *Down Beat*, and the very negative things they were saying about them. "This is anti-jazz. It's going to be the end of the universe when these guys play." This was about '61, '62.

I played trumpet at that time, but I wasn't playing jazz. I didn't start playing jazz until, well, attempting to play jazz, until I went into the army in '63. There was a lot of music in Poughkeepsie. There were a lot clubs that had jazz on the weekend. I heard a band with friends from high school playing. I thought, "The next time I see these guys I'm going to be playing, too." While I was in the army I met some musicians who introduced me to the first piece of written jazz music I ever saw, which was Miles Davis's "Four." Then we had an opportunity to rehearse every day from eight to five in the evening. I was also enamored of Rahsaan Roland Kirk, so I used to try to play two trumpets at once. My band master told me I was the most insipid trumpet player he'd ever seen and that I would amount to nothing, and if I didn't get on the stick, man, he was going to put me out of the band and into the infantry. We weren't supposed to play jazz, because that was too disruptive. But we did anyway.

When I came home from the army I had been looking for Albert Ayler. I heard about him and read about him, but I had never heard his music. I went to New York and there was a record shop on Eighth Street and I saw the ESP album called *Bells*, which is one-sided. It's got a silkscreen painting on one side and you can see through it, it's clear plastic. So I'm looking at that and a voice over my shoulder said, "What do you think about that record?" I said, "I don't know, it certainly looks interesting and I can't wait to hear it." He said, "Well, that's my brother. I'm a trumpet player." It was Don Ayler. I said, "Oh? I'm a trumpet player, too. I just got out of the army and I've been really looking forward to hearing this." He said, "Well, why don't you come to a rehearsal." He wrote down the address and said, "We're going to be at such and such a place and why don't you come?" I said, "You know, I really would like to, but I don't live here. I live in Poughkeepsie." So I never went.

It was the sound of Albert's music that piqued my interest in the saxophone. I was working in a factory. I worked there about eighteen years. It paid my bills and it allowed me to travel. They went on strike. The strike lasted for two years and I had a lot of free time, so I borrowed a saxophone.

I went to the clubs where I used to play my trumpet and tried to play sax. They told me never to come back with that thing. That was in March of '68. By September of '68 I gave my first concert and I played the saxophone. By April of '69 I had my first recording as a leader and I played my saxophone. I've been playing it ever since.

My ideas grew and my listening experience grew. It was really difficult to find people to play the kind of music that I wanted to play. They were more interested in straightahead stuff. Curiously, I think a lot of them are still playing today the same kind of music that they were playing in 1962. I just know what made me most comfortable, what I was hearing and what I was feeling. What they were doing for me was the past and what I was hearing as a result of exposure to Ornette and Eric Dolphy, in particular, seemed to be the future. I was also interested in people like Harry Partch.

* * *

In July of 1967 I was invited to make a recording with Clifford Thornton in New York. I was in a building on Barrow Street and it turned out that Ornette had an apartment just across from where I was rehearsing. And while I was there he heard me playing the trumpet, I was in a room by myself, and a knock came on the door and it was Ornette. I opened the door and there he was with a trumpet and my mouth just dropped. He said, "Here, try this. I heard your playing, try this. I got to go to Fort Worth to visit my family. I'm going to be away for about a week. When you're finished with it, just put it back in the room." He gave it to me and turned around and left. I took it and tried a few notes on it and said, "This can't be happening. I can't do this." When I was sure he was gone I put it back.

The next day I had to drive back to Poughkeepsie. As I was driving back it came on the radio that John Coltrane had died. I think the funeral was the 21st of July, on a Friday. The 22nd of July was our recording session scheduled in Brooklyn, a Saturday. I went back down to that apartment on that Friday for rehearsal and again a knock came on the door. It was Ornette and he said, "Are you going to John Coltrane's funeral?" I said, "Well, I hadn't planned to. I don't have the right clothes." He said, "You don't need clothes, you just go." I said, "Okay." I went and I was there. I heard Ornette's band playing, I heard Albert Ayler's band playing, and I came outside. I was standing outside St. Peter's Church on Lenox Avenue. Ornette came out with Billy Higgins and a drummer named Harold Avent. He saw me and he said, "We're going to the cemetery, do you want to go?" I said, "Yeah, sure." Up comes a limousine, a Cadillac. We jump in it and off we head to the cemetery in Long Island. But we get stuck in traffic and by the time we get to the cemetery the service is all over. There we are. Ornette's standing there over Coltrane's grave, no photographers. I don't think anybody has a picture of that.

Later that night, Ornette was playing at the [Village] Vanguard with his trio and he said, "Come on over." One of the last pieces they played that night was John Coltrane's "Naima." I don't know if Ornette ever released the recording, but I know he had one because he had this little Nagra tape recorder with a reel to reel. He recorded everything. I was like a groupie for Ornette for a while. [laughs] I'd go around carrying his saxophone. After the Vanguard gig we were walking down Seventh Ave., stopping at some chicken joint to get a sandwich on the way back to Barrow Street. He was great.

* * *

Last year I got to play with Milford Graves, the drummer who played with Albert Ayler's band at John Coltrane's funeral. Milford is amazing. The year before, Christopher Wool had an exhibition at the Guggenheim. He became enamored of my *Nation Time* recording and made a special painting with the same title, which was placed at the top of the Guggenheim. I was invited to play there with the Scandinavian band, The Thing. Later, Christopher had a second exhibition in Chicago and I was invited to play a duo set with Milford. I thought, "Wow this is really great, until the gravity of what I agreed to hit me—Oh dear God, I'm going to play with Milford Graves! What am I going to do?"

Milford's drums were brought to Chicago in a specially prepared truck as an art object. Milford wanted to talk about music, but I didn't want to do that so I went off to a party to clear my head for the next day. Just before the sound check, I got a text on my phone, "Shall we go completely crazy tonight?" I replied, "Well, I'm doing my stretching exercises and I'll be ready to fly." Milford's response was, "We should fly on wings of inspiration." I thought, "Wow, this is great." Now comes time for the sound check. Milford's incredible drum set is on stage and he's setting it all up and talking all the while. Then, he begins to tell me how much he hates saxophone players. [laughs] We had just met earlier so I knew it wasn't anything personal. It was just, "Sax players play too loud, they play too many notes."

I'm thinking, "Oh God, now what's going to happen?" I only had my tenor sax. We go to our dressing room and when we are announced Milford comes out dressed all in white, like the martial artist that he is, and I'm dressed all in black like Batman. There we are, yin and yang on the stage, and it begins. He started playing and he's singing at the same time. I'm not going to step on him, so I just closed my eyes and I played. It's taken me over a year to even listen to a recording of the concert, because I was afraid it was going to be horrible, that I didn't make the grade. Finally, about a month ago I heard it and it's really something. I just blanked out in the process. We played and I couldn't remember what we played or how it went or how long it was. It was just, "I'm here and this is what I'm going to do. This is all I can do. I'm limited. I'm going to do the best I can. But will it be good enough?" I hope the recording will be released; all of those questions will be answered.

Welf Dorr | Michael Bogdanffy-Kriegh

Leave the Window Open
Welf Dorr Unit

"One good minute could last you the whole year"
—Superchunk, "The First Part"

The centerpiece of the stage is the lava lamp Christmas tree. It's tall and plastic and illuminated, lights slowly changing colors, rising and falling, undulating like a jellyfish. I'm not saying I want one at home, but here it belongs.

Welf Dorr grins beneath a pork pie hat. He's a jovial host, genuinely amused and motivated by his bandmates. He's also fond of his effects, delay and phaser. Watching him hold his alto sax with one hand, twiddle and modulate with the other, brings me back to my prog rock days. A little Rick Wakeman approach to accompany the Johnny Carson.

Something I heard about the Welf Dorr Unit has me ready for sharp sounds that jut out, get caught on anything that happens by. That will come later. In the meantime, Dorr and guitarist Dave Ross surf whole notes awash in their effects boxes. Ross has dozens of credits on his website. He lists the numerous types of music he's played over the years, among them punk *and* hardcore. It's a subtle variation but it merits bonus points, like that line from *The Blues Brothers*: "We have both kinds of music, country *and* western."

* * *

"Most people don't live in a place where interesting things happen frequently. Invariably, in all of these places, there is a small clutch of people who are absolutely dedicated to making their community more fun and exciting. They just want to do their part, and make the place where they live a little less drab and soul crushing. This is a constant. These are the people who start bands and put on shows and form roller derby leagues and run little record labels out of their kitchen and all manner of other constructive activities. Generally, they make no money. They struggle against daunting odds, just so their community has sounds other than the monotonous churn of factory equipment and the mundane clack of computer keyboards one cubicle over, and sights other than Subway signs and Chevy dealerships." —Rev. Nørb, writer, musician

* * *

James Keepnews is among that small clutch of people. He's been booking shows since he was in college and across subsequent moves to New York City, Albany, Peekskill, Jersey City, and Cold Spring before landing in Beacon.

* * *

Dorr breaks out a bass clarinet, increases the sonic distance with Ross. Drummer Joe Hertenstein swells on the cymbals, cresting but not crashing. Along with the traditional collection of cymbals—hi-hat, crash, ride— he's added some unusual characters. One is a 5" mini-cymbal mounted on his hi-hat stand. Another cymbal battered and torn, dangles like the sword of Damocles from a rack tom mount. It looks like shrapnel. I don't know how he avoids slicing himself every time his arms pass near it.

* * *

Yesterday my daughter and I went to Dia for her first museum visit. Maggie was amped up. She wanted to draw everything she saw and write captions and copy down the artists' names. I followed as she walked from one exhibit to the next. Then we came to Robert Smithson's "Map of Broken Glass (Atlantis)." As the title implies, it's made of broken glass. What the title leaves out is that the glass is laid out on the floor, piled long and wide (twenty feet by fifteen) and high (a good foot, foot and a half). I trust that craft was involved, that there was ample deliberation. But it's still broken glass on the floor. A trap ready to spring. There's no border, no barrier. It's us and the glass. The late Smithson claimed "map." I say "menacing mound." It creeped me out. Maggie took her time. She laughed. She sketched. She wrote, "Glass! Glass! Run away!"

I did my best not to rush her along but even as we walked away I kept looking back. I knew the mass wasn't going to mobilize. I assumed no one would trip and fall. Still, I looked back just to check.

* * *

Joe Hertenstein dodges tragedy time and again, avoids clashing with that cymbal. He locks in with bassist Dmitry Ishenko. I expect Dorr and Ross to follow suit, succumb to the rhythm section's gravitational pull. But they resist, persist with their cough syrup ways.

Dorr holds for a bar here, two there. He adjusts the effects boxes, though less often. Ross leans back and into the sound. They stake out the relative calm at the center of the storm, reveling in the subtle, unresolved tension. This could easily go wrong, but it's less like a ballgame that ends in a tie and more like a short story with an ambiguous ending; there's work to do, things to sort out. Ishenko motors on. Hertenstein swings. They're headed for the conventional when Ross counters with an angular approach, launching shards of guitar, Sonny Sharrock-style. James walks past and mouths, "Wow."

Michael Bogdanffy-Kriegh is among that small clutch, too. He's been posting photos from Quinn's for weeks. James introduces us and Michael and I compare reactions to these Monday nights. He says what I haven't been able to articulate: "I didn't know this was my kind of music until I heard it."

* * *

"A funny thing happens when good people work hard at something: it turns out pretty great." —Jennifer Whiteford, *Punk Parenthood for the Sleep Deprived*

* * *

The next number is a different tale. Dorr introduces it as a "free take on Mal Waldron's 'Left Alone.'" Despite the tune's keyboard origins this version belongs to Ross. In short order he ramps up and sails a sea of pyrotechnics. Dorr smiles, laughs, looks for someone to respond. He turns to Ishenko, whose eyes are closed. Dorr scans the crowd, seeking a "Can you believe this?" connection.

Between songs Dorr introduces the band. He lingers on Ishenko, whose style is easygoing, from his right hand resting on the body of his bass to his glasses/beard/Chaucer-thesis-brewing-in-the-back-of-the-brain mien. Some take life in stride. Others, like Ishenko, do so standing still.

"We thought he was Russian, but he's Ukrainian. We seriously thought of renaming the band Free Ukraine." (Was that a collective groan or am

I projecting my sense that it's too soon in light of the social unrest in Ukraine? Is Dorr the Gilbert Gottfried of the jazz circuit?)

The band is even better in the second set. (How often does that happen here, the first set paving the way for the second? Onset and rhyme. Set up and punch line.) There are fewer effects in "Flowers for Albert," more traction, more grit, with Ross scratching funky accents and Hertenstein thumping a cowbell. The slow, gradual landing gets better as it downshifts, the music mixing with clinking pint glasses and laughter.

For the closer Hertenstein places that menacing sword of Damocles of a cymbal on the end of a stick and spins it, twirls the damn thing. I'm relieved when he tosses it to the floor. There are hollers for an encore and James closes up shop. "If it's a Monday night, there's great music here at Quinn's."

Jason Kao Hwang | Michael Bogdanffy-Kriegh

This Big River
Jason Kao Hwang & Satoshi Takeishi

"Develop the film of your life / Right now"
—Guided By Voices, "Vote for Me, Dummy"

Elapsed time – 0:00

James Keepnews strides to the stage and introduces the musicians, Jason Kao Hwang (violin, viola, electronics) and Satoshi Takeishi (drums, electronics). Unlike most Monday nights at Quinn's, which offer two sets, this will be a "special one-long-set night," which will be one long piece.

Takeishi turns the snare off and wields mallets, blurring the distinction among drums. Hwang runs his violin through an effects box. I look away and momentarily mistake it for a guitar. Takeishi fades out and Hwang delves into deep slides. He clicks his sticks against the rim of the kick drum, seemingly drops and fumbles them over the edges of the snare and toms, like a series of one-time motions, impossible to replicate. But then he repeats the sequence, manages to retrace his steps.

* * *

Driving to the show I see the slightest sliver of a crescent moon. It looks oddly familiar, that moon, smiling down from the bruised skyline that rests above the shadowed trees. The excitement for tonight's show has me assigning meaning to everything. I feel like Neil from *The Young Ones*.

* * *

Elapsed time – 5:00

Takeishi reaches to the laptop on his left. Despite a clear sight line I can't connect his motions and his sounds—what I see and what I hear are at odds with each other. Meanwhile Hwang is out of sight—I literally can't see him. I have no idea who's producing what and yet the further they go, the more sense it makes, the more things coalesce. Hwang trades a bow for plucking and Takeishi reemerges, laid back, then fading up on a kick/snare conversation.

* * *

I parked in front of the Beacon Wine Shoppe. There's always a spot there. I suspect the "Condemned" sign posted on the front door helps. There's a group of firefighters at the corner and light spilling from the adjacent street. It's movie set-bright or, more likely, scene-of-a-fire bright.

"OK to park here?" I ask.

"Oh yeah, they're tearing the building down tomorrow. Finally letting us do some roof training."

* * *

I think of the moonlit sky again and realize where I've seen that image before: it's the smile on the book jacket for *The Hitchhiker's Guide to the Galaxy*.

* * *

Geoff Dyer wrote that looking forward to a show is better than the actual show. Anticipation eclipses experience. He was writing about rock concerts. What he said was this: "Nothing that happens subsequently can live up to those opening moments when all the power suddenly erupts, and you, emphatically, are no longer waiting for something to begin. Pretty soon, though, you are waiting for it to end."

* * *

Elapsed time – 10:00

Hwang is sweeping his bow wildly from side to side, violently hacking away at his instrument. He bends this way, bops that. He must be producing a tremendous amount of friction—how hot is the hair on that bow?—yet maintains his composure.

* * *

Dyer was writing about a Def Leppard concert, a purely commercial enterprise, a cash grab. That's fine. No judgment, not from someone whose E.L.O. collection is within arm's reach. But it is different. Commercial music is like eating at Burger King, the craving, the fleeting consumption. Too often such experiences leave me with regret or in denial.

* * *

Today is Opening Day for the Mets. My anticipation for the new season hasn't hit fever pitch, but it's rising. It'll only climb as spring transitions into summer.

First pitch is 1:10. In between classes I check the score online. The Mets put up a 3-0 lead against the Nationals' Stephen Strasburg. By the time dismissal drags around, the Mets have blown two leads and cling to a narrow 5-4 advantage with two outs in the ninth.

The classroom empties and I follow the game pitch by pitch. The Mets' Bobby Parnell faces Denard Span. Foul ball. Ball. Foul ball. Ball. Repeat until Span doubles in the tying run. Minutes into the first game of the season and the roller coaster is already whipping me about.

* * *

I've had experiences like Dyer's, events that I'd rather think about before they unfold than live through. None come to mind today. Not the Mets game. Certainly not what Hwang and Takeishi are conjuring.

* * *

Elapsed time – 15:00

For the first time, Hwang settles into a recognizable pattern. It's pleasing, though eerie. The repetition suggests a movie, a quiet countryside shot that pulls back to reveal a car chase, demise imminent.

* * *

Leaving work I flip on the radio and catch the Mets score—Washington 9, New York 5—just before they cut to commercial. I reach for the volume as a couple begins arguing over whose burger has crispier bacon. Is this how we react in the face of tragedy? The Mets are choking, have choked, blown their first chance of the new year and all we get are soggy pork products?

* * *

Are the Mets a Burger King team? Is following baseball a Burger King pastime?

* * *

Elapsed time – 20:00

I'm lost in a strangely satisfying way; I can't keep track of what's transpiring. Like a surveyor without a theodolite, I can't monitor the vertical or horizontal planes. I'm not sure how much orientation matters at the moment.

On the way home I listen to Hwang's CD, *Symphony of Souls*. It's credited to a forty-piece orchestra billed as the Spontaneous River. The name reminds me of a Mike Watt quote. Speaking of an early Minutemen record he said, "They [the songs on *The Punch Line*] weren't supposed to stand on their own. They're supposed to be part of this big river." Hwang and Takeishi harness a similar dynamic.

* * *

Elapsed time – 25:00

Takeishi taps away on his laptop. He samples and loops Hwang's violin. James Keepnews swoops in, excitedly sharing that this is real-time sampling. Meanwhile Takeishi picks up his sticks. He solos, darting in and out, around the snare. With his left foot he maintains a swing beat on the hi-hat. It's a one-person dialogue: his drumming is out there, free, while his use of cymbals is traditional. A perfect example of how complementary these styles can be.

* * *

A counter argument—one that supports Dyer's point—is that Hwang and Takeishi's performance is an extended, heightened sense of anticipation. We're stuck in a state of "What's next?" What's coming up is greater than what is. This show, this piece of music, is so rousing. Every nerve ending feels open and aware. What's best is what's now.

* * *

Elapsed time – 30:00

Hwang reverts to the wah wah sound. Takeishi is right there every step of the way.

A few years ago, watching the Milwaukee band the Catholic Boys, my friend Pete said the band's drummer played lead drums—not just rhythm, not just solos, but lead drums. Takeishi has that.

* * *

Another counterargument: it's a matter of tension vs. release. The anticipation, the buildup, is the tension. The experience, the event, is the release. Tonight's session alters that. The tension is in the experience, the event, and there's no release in sight. That's what sustains it.

* * *

Elapsed time – 35:00

There is a momentary nod to classical music, albeit a buzzing, swarming sound as Hwang dive bombs between the peaks and valleys of his violin's register. After the show he says, "We generate wild mood swings."

Even though I'm watching the clock, I've lost track of the passage of time. The hands move but the numbers don't carry much meaning, passing through my field of view like mile markers on a late night drive.

* * *

Elapsed time – 40:00

Enter the gong. It's a small gong, the size of a salad plate. Takeishi holds it while still playing with a mallet in each hand. He bangs the gong against the other drums, then pulls it across the snare and floor tom. Forty minutes in and Takeishi is still pulling tricks out of his bag.

So is Hwang. His sound rockets to eleven. It's piercing, too loud, ringing my ears. It's the first sign of excess and it bear traps our attention. There's applause from the tables in back. The counter crowd is stunned. We're still except for the guy two seats over who shakes his head in disbelief.

* * *

Elapsed time – 45:00

Hwang sets aside his bow and plucks again. Takeishi runs the length of a drumstick along the edge of his ride cymbal. It's subtle but he manages to sample it with the mic mounted above his kit. His ability to cast a narrow, targeted net is remarkable. More like spearing, I suppose.

* * *

Elapsed time – 50:00

Takeishi switches to brushes. Hwang to viola. It's as if he is playing backward. Like an optical illusion, I can see his right hand move one way yet his sound moves another. I wish I'd paid more attention in high school physics.

* * *

Elapsed time – 55:00

Hwang plays, then pauses. The show is nearly over. I haven't thought of it until now, haven't wanted the performance to end, but Hwang and Takeishi are clearly about to close.

* * *

Takeishi sets down his sticks and rests. Hwang finishes, slowly, quietly, tenderly, closing the cover at the end of a great novel. It's over and far better than expected.

Michael Bisio | Michael Bogdanffy-Kriegh

On Accordions and Tubby Time
Accortet

"Tradition is a trap"
—Hussalonia, "o rlly?"

Here's what I expect: I'm going to be late. I'm going to miss the first set, and my regret will deepen as I hear about what I've missed.

Here's what I encounter: I arrive mid-song, in the midst of a frame-by-frame detonation, a mushroom cloud creeping across the room. Something has gone off, and its aftermath has yet to hit.

Photographer Michael Bogdanffy-Kriegh is crouched low, stage right. His lens leads my eye to the stage, where Accortet leader Michael Bisio is bent at the waist, feverishly bowing, burrowing into the deepest recesses of his bass. His actions are large, demonstrative. On a dime he turns, carefully, deliberately, an archeologist gently brushing an artifact. What is Bisio looking for down there? Escape? Salvation? Something just beyond his grasp?

Everyone is tuned in, waiting to see what he'll unearth next. I back up, take a seat by the door. There's no way I'm walking through this moment.

* * *

In *One Week* Buster Keaton and Sybil Seely play newlyweds. They've just received an "assemble your own home" kit, but the parts have been mislabeled. The house comes out all wrong. Everything is there, but askew. Acute and obtuse angles reside where right angles are intended; the house is an abstract marvel. Keaton and Seely may have used traditional tools and materials but they've built something decidedly unconventional.

* * *

Rounding out Accortet's lineup are Kirk Knuffke (cornet), Art Bailey (accordion), and Michael Wimberly (drums). That kind of instrumentation has "traditional" written all over it, in fountain pen, especially the accordion. Accordions evoke Lawrence Welk. But Weird Al, too, so who knows. After weeks of Quinn's indoctrination, I listen longer before deciding. I trust that Accortet will use these tools to traverse nontraditional sounds. It's a matter of how.

* * *

"Getting a little work done?" The guy next to me sees my notebook. I explain and he introduces himself as Ronnie. The band winds down a Thelonious Monk tune, "Ask Me Now," cool and invigorating like the spring air that eases through the front door. "Cozy on a Monday night," Ronnie says.

That's true. Accortet are. Or at least they can be. They can also stir it up with originals like Bisio's "Giant Chase." And while Bisio consistently exudes a big personality, so do the other band members. Wimberly gives the quartet its rhythmic foundation, while Knuffke cements their diffuse sounds, and Bailey furnishes a variety of exteriors.

Ronnie has been buying instruments at yard sales, starting to play drums again, a little cornet, too. He's got a place where he can play these days. He asks if I was here for the Joe McPhee show. And the Jason Kao Hwang show. And the Mike Dopazo show. What he's saying but not stating is that these Monday nights make him want to play again, pick up old habits, make something.

* * *

For a long time I based my perception of Beacon on two local institutions: Pete Seeger and Dia. Folk art and fine art. These shows draw from both. They start early and they're free. The musicians are approachable, down to earth, more like DIY punk rockers in terms of their art > commerce outlook. And the music is consistently absorbing, challenging in the right ways.

James introduces me to drummer Michael Wimberly, who possesses that rare combination of accomplishment and humility. Anyone with P-Funk and Henry Rollins credits has reason to boast. He mentions neither, instead asking what I'm writing. The conversation turns to punk rock and he talks about his days with the Pony Boys in Cleveland— "the ties, the hair, the make-up"; the singer who sailed through a liquor store window; opening for the Ramones, being booed. Through the chaos, Wimberly was making his way through school, spending his time with flashcards, "studying French or whatever." A few minutes with Wimberly is like a tour of time, place, and genre; he's played it all. I say that I've always assumed that anyone who can play jazz can play anything. He sips, smiles, and laughs. "Nope."

He describes Bisio's songs as "compositions with room." He tends to lay back tonight, but he knows when to open it up, especially in the closing song, his arms crossing back and forth between the cymbals. (James: "Oh yeah, the windshield wipers. Gotta clear it away!")

Cornetist Knuffke has that sense, too. His tone can be delightfully airy, like when he and Bisio duet on "Living Large," finding the space between and within the notes. He can push up the faders, too, crank it out sharp and cutting. (It's Knuffke's birthday and later he's serenaded and treated to a candle-in-a-rice-ball, which is the first of two Quinn's traditions that I learn about tonight.) Knuffke holds one whole note after another, the rhythm section percolates and Bailey, whom Bisio calls the band's "esteemed accordion-ista," interjects. He grins but never smirks, keeps kitsch at arm's length. It helps that Bailey's look—Fu Manchu moustache, long sleeve flannel, professor glasses—reminds me of Mike Watt.

* * *

Bisio doesn't say much from stage, but his circuitous setups are humorous. "I say stuff but I wish I didn't. Here's a song I wrote for Henry Grimes.[2] He's a hero of mine. I wrote it for him when he was still dead. He got alive. It's still okay to play it now. First there'll be a drum solo. Then I'll play a G."

His subsequent solo is exceptional. I've never seen a human strike an object with greater force. I cringe watching him bash the bass strings. How can any callus withstand that? The splattering of blood across his white shirt must be imminent, at the very least the rupturing of a blister or three. The outcome seems secondary to the effort, the sweat.

Glass is half full = Mortality's got nothing on Bisio, not now.

---

2 Grimes was a first call bassist throughout the '50s and '60s. He vanished in the late '60s, was thought to have died, only to resurface thirty-five years later and resume performing.

Glass is half empty = Sisyphus. The strings, the pain, whatever he's attempting to push away, is only going to recoil. Why bother?

I vote for the former. Bisio – 1, The Void – 0.

* * *

I notice James announces fewer upcoming shows during the closing credits, and last I checked there aren't any shows listed yet for next month. I hope there's nothing to this but for now I decide to stay later, get caught up in the post-show conversations. The night winds down as King Tubby wafts from the PA. Apparently I've been leaving just before the start of Tubby Time, the second Quinn's tradition I experience tonight. The juxtaposition with Accortet says, *Recognize this as your wakeup call, it's time to leave.* But the hypnotic, narcotic sounds say, *Stay, relax, the work day is hours away.*

Alan "Juice" Glover | Michael Bogdanffy-Kriegh

I Am a Scientist
The Juice Glover Quartet

"I'm a jazz musician, but I'm allowed to think."
—Juice Glover

Keyboardist Lora Cohan opens "Of Things Green," warm and inviting; gets the blood pumping. The rest of the band listens, heads bowed, motionless. Then up and swinging, quick and sure footed, like a middleweight. Saxophonist Alan "Juice" Glover is gliding along, sailing. But don't think "The doctor will see you" jazz. Glover has an edge, a sound that enlivens rather than anaesthetizes.

* * *

I've been telling my neighbor about these Monday night sessions. Keith almost made it tonight, but something came up at the last minute and he tells me definitely some other time. I don't doubt his sincerity, but worry the series is coming to an end. There are no shows listed for next month, and the full slate has usually been posted by now. Has the plug been pulled? Have the numbers been crunched and we're headed for tribute bands and trivia nights?

* * *

For weeks James has been telling me about Glover, incredulous that I've not heard of him, more insistent than usual that I attend this show. Before the music begins I check out the merch table, which is covered with CDs and DVDs, and a brochure for an invention of Glover's, the Musiversal Visual Aid. Eric Porter, a friend of Glover's, recognizes my deer-in-headlights look and offers to help. He walks me through the various artifacts and Glover's backstory.

Glover has been active since the '70s. An electrician by trade, he's been performing for decades. He's also published a book and directed a short film, *Birth*. He began filming in 1969 but financial constraints postponed production and he wound up storing the film stock in a refrigerator for three years. After he finished editing, courtesy of afterhours sessions at CBS, it was another four years before he was able to record the soundtrack. Meanwhile, he hosted shows at his loft in Alphabet City, The Firehouse Theatre, mentoring the likes of bassist William Parker.

Glover has lived in nearby Poughkeepsie for years. I can't believe a talent of this magnitude lives just over the hills and I've never heard of him. I find myself backing into an Obi-Wan Kenobi comparison—the wise, mysterious elder about whose legendary exploits the locals know little.

* * *

In Josh Wilker's *Benchwarmer*, he describes the "order and wonder and calm" that came from seeing Henry Aaron's name at the beginning of every baseball encyclopedia he read as a kid. As he grew older the rest of Wilker's life changed in ways both predictable and unimaginable but Aaron's name always led off, was first, something on which he could rely.

* * *

Glover is a showman; he could hold a stage without an instrument. He quotes *Hamlet*. ("'To be or not to be'—scholars don't really know what it means but I do. You'll have to read my memoirs.") He sells the challenges of improvising over 10/8 time, makes it sound like a deeply gratifying challenge.

Prior to the show I read about Glover online. A few sources cite his Christian faith. From my experience, however limited, Christian musicians preach more than examine. The term "spiritual jazz" is also used in reference to Glover. That's more apt. Glover inquires more than lectures. "*Here's what I'm grappling with...*" This is Glover as John Coltrane.

* * *

Years later, pitcher David Aardsma "slouched toward a major league mound for the first time" and supplanted Henry Aaron at the top of the baseball alphabet. Wilker describes the unsettling realization that something on which he'd relied was no longer there, one more example of how "the world kept getting more unsortable."

* * *

Glover is a free thinker, inclined toward big questions. Sure, he'll preach, get in his three cents on things theological. He sets up "Be Still and Know That I Am" by talking about Jesus and Luke. But he also reads the room well and knows when to press on.

"I admire scientists. They have a thought. They work on it. Then they try again." Setting up the title track from *The Blue Shift,* Glover wonders if there was more than one Big Bang. "He couldn't be satisfied with *a* bang. It's more like bang di di bang da bang bang." The same joke is printed on the back of *The Blue Shift* CD. I love performers who know when and how to reuse material. Glover as Don Rickles.

* * *

When I was younger I feared losing things of all sizes—from being called on in class or leaving my baseball glove out in the rain, to my family moving or my parents divorcing. I was afraid that who or what I cherished—people, privacy, possessions—would be taken away. Similar anxieties sometimes still cling like bird ox, garden variety worries that stick more than they should. I pull them off, pretty sure I've picked off all the bits, but they persist.

* * *

Glover explains the underlying science of *The Blue Shift*. It's a "hypothetical history of time and space" part of which entails what red shifts reveal about the expansion of the universe. He ponders what blue shifts will reveal. The songs from this record make more sense, he says, when you listen to them in order. It's like he jumped into a mid-semester astronomy lecture. "I started with the sixth track on the album," Glover says, "that's unfair." (To which someone responds, "It's okay, we're advanced around here.") Glover as Carl Sagan.

* * *

Each month I look at the list of upcoming shows, check out the acts online, mark the calendar with the dates I can make. A couple of weeks ago I noticed that new shows weren't being added and I've been reluctant to ask about the details. These shows are too good to be true and I don't want to know if they're ending.

* * *

Taken out of context these anecdotes might frame Glover as a purveyor of "folksy wisdom," someone with scratch-off thinking—little depth and easy to brush aside. His Musiversal Slide Rule, among other things, says otherwise. Billed as a "Circular Slide Rule," it's an impressive artifact for laypeople. For musicians, whose testimonials fill the brochure, it's a functional tool, using shapes and colors to represent different chords. It's ingenious. I think of how hard we strive in schools to make concepts accessible to kids, scaffold and differentiate, and here is someone who's translated sound to polygons and primary colors. Glover enjoys discussing the underlying math. "The lower the ratio, the more harmonious, more pleasing to the ear," he says, reaching for one of the discs.

With all the talk of inner and outer space, it'd make sense for Glover and company to play slow and contemplative, allow everything to sink in. There are aspects of that. Lora Cohan keeps finding gaps to fill. Bassist William Hopson displays new levels of laid back, breaking character, smiling, only when Glover mentions his upcoming wedding.

But while Cohan and Hopson keep things grounded, drummer Michael T. A. Thompson takes off, keeping the beat and soloing around it simultaneously. Rare is the drummer with so much vertical action, it's like discovering a new Romance language—the fundamentals are familiar while the phrasing and accents and combinations are singular.

Glover plays with a propulsion that belies his years. He's about to celebrate "the seventeenth anniversary of my fiftieth birthday" and has a number of ideas on the drawing board. He has a new album of originals brewing, including *Paradox on a Narrow Road* ("a multi-mixed metaphor including how improvisers lean on one another") and his kids want him to record a Christmas record ("in your style," they say).

* * *

James takes the mic amidst the applause. "This is my thirtieth night curating shows at Quinn's…" My heart plummets. I fear that this is the end-of-an era confirmation I'd dreaded, and yet that ellipsis hangs in the air. The shows are changing behind the scenes but not ending. James announces that they will continue, though at different intervals and with other promoters pitching in. Relieved, I seek out Eric for advice on which CDs to buy.

James Keepnews | Steve Ventura

James Keepnews, musician, curator of the Monday Night Jazz Sessions and Extreme Thursdays

The weird underground, it comes in so many shapes and sizes and directions. I think back to hearing classical music of an avant garde type when I was in grade school. I didn't have anything to compare it to and felt lost in a certain way. A lot of it has to do with just being a misfit as an adolescent. You know, like you're never going to get invited to the parties, you stay home alone, and you're listening to the left side of the radio stations. In the early '80s, things like WNYU, on weekend nights they played the craziest things. I heard Captain Beefheart, even comparatively straight-ahead things like Robyn Hitchcock, some of his solo stuff. I had a good friend in high school who was crazy into punk rock. I didn't really know much about it at all. He would turn me on to comps like *Not So Quiet on the Western Front*, which contained countless things, including Dead Kennedys ["A Child and His Lawn Mower"], "Dan with the Mellow Hair" [by Naked Lady Wrestlers]. I remember crazy stuff off of that. But I thought if I shaved my head and wore a T-shirt, I just felt like I couldn't wear that uniform. That was going to mean I was more of a conformist. Punk means thinking for yourself.

And I loved prog rock! I was crazy into punk rock, but I loved Emerson, Lake & Palmer. King Crimson was enormous. I ended up with their collection *Young Person's Guide to King Crimson* after they broke up in the '70s. It had this booklet that compiled reviews they'd gotten over the years. Mel Collins was in the band—as far as I'm concerned the best saxophonist in the history of rock music period—and they'd say "Sometimes he can really play outside and do these Aylerish solos." So suddenly I got to find Ayler. Ayler who? What's this? Who? What? Where? So, I'm finding more about Albert Ayler and free jazz.

I volunteered for this cultural not-for-profit, the Lower Eastside Community Music Workshop that Jemeel Moondoc was a co-founder of. They did things at El Bohio, which was this old high school just east of Tompkins Square Park. During the Giuliani era they finally sold it, and some developer wanted to clear it out. But for a long time it was a squat, just an abandoned school. All these education institutions were in there and CHARAS, this underground film collective, was there. Amazing things. It was the summer of 1987 and I volunteered for them. Had a chance to hear Roy Campbell, Jemeel, Charles Gayle, meeting William Parker, all these people. I had been doing jazz radio at Hamilton College. When you hear these guys, and you're removed from it—you've only got the records and the liner notes—and you haven't seen them live, they become this Olympian cast, this pantheon of gods.

Come to find out, going to these concerts, if you're lucky, they get ten people in the audience. They make no money. I don't know how they made rent back then. I'd be thinking, "Jeez, how do these guys do it?" Just completely brought me down to earth and made me realize how hard it is to be playing good music and decide, "I'm going to be broke, I'm going to have to find some way to make money if I want to make *any* money at all." And it's not going to have anything to do with trying to put it on the music, if you want to play in an uncompromising way. That was very revealing to me. Made me all the more supportive.

I'll never forget, John Zorn was on WNYC being interviewed and they played about five hardcore tunes all lasting maybe a minute. The DJ was like, "Okay, John, why'd you play that?" He said, "As a composer, there's something about hardcore in its directness, in its simplicity, and its structural elements. A hardcore tune together has all these elements that I embrace in great classical music or great music anywhere. Very interesting composition. Challenging to the ear and exciting." He articulated something that I couldn't. You ever listen to Naked City? They slam it up against each other. There's also that element of outsider art, anti-commercialism that's always going to have these awesome Venn diagrams.

In 1987, I was bringing up a lot of music to Hamilton College. I brought up The Group. Billy Bang, Ahmed Abdullah, the late great Marion Brown, Sirone—amazing bassist, that cat was amazing—and Andrew Cyrille. They did two sets, very avant garde. Compositional but very free, a lot of room. They played two sets and got two standing ovations both sets. They were psyched. They're coming from the Lower East Side, playing to ten people, most of whom they know or have seen, not making any money. To come upstate and get a rapturous reception and get paid a little bit, get shown around, get wined and dined. But more importantly, they got over to an audience in a big way. As I was driving them back to their hotel Andrew Cyrille said, "I've always said we don't have to compromise this music at all. We don't have to do anything to sweeten it, make it more palatable to mainstream sensibilities. We just have to present it as our art, as it is, and people with ears are going to hear it."

The environment [at Quinn's] is great. The musicians get a good gig, they get an audience that really wants to listen to it, and is even being converted too. People are not walking in with a deep understanding of the history of this music or what it's about, but like what they hear. I'm trying to make it work out so that these guys can get good gigs and people have a chance to hear them. Increasingly, man, I feel like it's my life's work to do as much as I can. It's not even an evangelical thing. I mean, there is a vibe of that, but it's not like, "*You* need to listen to this!" It's more like, "This is happening, listen to it."

The Ties That Bind
Michael Kadnar

"I sometimes stagger but, sugar, I seldom fall"
—Kris Kristofferson, "Smokey Put the Sweat on Me"

A band of dark blue tops the western skyline, layers of white and purple beneath. Two titanic tubes of water cut across the grain, colossal cylinders of rain. But when I top the next hill the sunset is beautiful and blinding, a tangerine fireball so perfect we should all pull over and gaze and sketch and fill notebooks with overly earnest poetry. The sort of sight that would inspire an issue of Seth's *Palookaville*.

* * *

In Todd Taylor's *The Insect King*, Murtaw is talked into attending a football game at his high school. At half-time he's spellbound by the spectacle of the Gold Sequined Girl. He can't figure her out and that's much of her appeal—"it's a form of not understanding that he liked."

Mondays at Quinn's are often like that, though tonight's different. I'm able to dial in to the band, a quartet led by drummer Michael Kadnar, before I sit down. Their timing and unity resonate immediately. Kadnar has a great touch on the ride cymbal, generous and deft. Sean Morrison and Joe Heider are up front. Morrison plays a Fender Rhodes electric piano, Heider an electric hollow body—two of my favorite sounds. Add in Harry D'Agostino on upright bass and I float back to Freddie Hubbard's band on *Straight Life*—Herbie Hancock, Ron Carter, Jack DeJohnette, and a young, pre-smooth George Benson.

* * *

Matt Kindt's *Mind Mgmt* obscures the divide between dreams and reality. In issue #19 an unnamed woman fronts as a bookstore employee driving books back and forth between stores. The true nature of her endeavors, however, is that she's a spy with the ability to "fall asleep and find people…courier messages through dreams." At least she's fairly certain this is the case. As the story unfolds she questions what's real and what's illusion. She's unsure whether she's a secret agent or a retail clerk with an overactive imagination.

* * *

Kadnar and company are a welcome reprieve from recent events. On Friday night the roof collapsed above my wife's business. The floors were flooded and she spent Saturday trying to contact the landlord and a series of overbooked plumbers and electricians. Then I found out that my mom may need another surgery for her arthritis, my friend Brian was assaulted walking home in Brooklyn, and James was held up at knifepoint a short walk from Quinn's.

* * *

One day, in that same issue of *Mind Mgmt*, the spy/clerk, driving from one store to the other, trying to puzzle out the true nature of her job, survives a car bomb. The experience shocks her, snaps her out of the ease of her daily routine. She gains a better understanding of her situation, thinking that she's not just "creating a world that I can fall into."

Am I doing something similar, creating a world that I can fall into by idealizing a scene and the town in which it's set? My friend Brett asked if the burgeoning scene at Quinn's is really that surprising given the relative proximity to New York City and the growing number of people relocating from Brooklyn. I live near but not in Beacon. I frequent but don't work at Quinn's. I'm spared the inevitable ego clashes and money squabbles, the cold shoulders and eye rolls that surely exist here as they do in any setting that strives to balance art and commerce.

* * *

James says he's still shaken but fine. People stop by our table, ask how he's doing, offer support, share their own versions of "gotta be careful in this town." Barney Fife parole officers bumble through one, SWAT team rigor defines another. Someone else chimes in, "Don't leave your phone on the counter. Mine got stolen last month."

There is too much swirling in my head and it takes awhile to recognize the changes to the front of the club. Several tables have been removed and the stage is wider. I like the new view, the wider screen. At first the side effects are minimal, just a couple of dumpster-bound tables by the entrance. But then, about halfway through the first set, Michael and his wife Holly walk past and sit in back. They always sit in front. Seeing them walk by and take a booth in back is like watching a catcher stroll past the pitcher's mound and set up in center field.

The night closes on an odd note. I've noticed an older gent walking back and forth, a ponytail halfway down his back, a saxophone case slung over his shoulder. I've been assuming that he's come from rehearsal and he's here, like the rest of us, to soak in the tunes. Between songs I notice him talking to the band. I can't gauge whether he's complimenting or goading them. In fact, he's asking to sit in. He announces himself as Huckleberry Infinity. He talks to Sean Morrison and I notice Joe Heider make eye contact with someone in the audience. Joe shrugs "What should we do?" and before we know it Mr. Infinity is playing. It's not necessary—Kadnar and company were doing just fine—but it's all right. Lends a Brautigan feel to the night—a twist, a wrinkle, a scrap that I don't know how to file. Though if this were a Brautigan story we'd close with the saxophone's perspective, slumbering in the dark, velvety confines of its case, dreaming of a childhood walk in the rain, waiting to sing again.

Donny Once More
Katherine Young's Pretty Monsters
Jessica Pavone

I knew I was loopy long before I missed the turn for Quinn's. I spent all yesterday outdoors in the sun, splashing around at a water park with my kids. Today I kept my classroom windows open all day, lulled by the light rain that just kept coming down.

Needless to say, I'm in the right frame of mind as Jessica Pavone warms up. Viola pinched between chin and neck she focuses on electronics, the gear at her feet. Tons of echo, slowly mounting. We watched *Mothra vs. Godzilla* over the weekend so I'm seeing monster movies as Pavone's pitches bend and shift.

She lets a minute or three pass before feeding new info to the effects box, lets it ring with the sounds of invading alien hordes. Usually that kind of work-to-noise ratio sends me fleeing, but Pavone knows when to pull up, switch back to the viola, push fresh sounds into the loop. My mental narrative cuts to grainy black and white footage of flying saucers storming Kentucky hollows at dusk.

Pavone plays for two beats, rests for two, rides one sound, then sets her sights on the next. The pace quickens and the feedback fluctuates, flickering images in an experimental film. It's the anti-solo solo, volume and texture trumping how many or how fast, huge blocks that jolt everything in the vicinity.

* * *

One of my students asked me to explain the difference between a stereotype and an archetype. I struggled for an answer. My immediate thought was that stereotypes make me squirm. Archetypes don't. I resist stereotypes. I try not to traffic in them, and I don't want to personify them. Me, the bearded, bespectacled white guy taking notes at a jazz show, thinks he rises above stereotypes, while sipping from a tulip glass of Belgian ale with a folded newspaper at the ready, sitting alongside a tattooed long hair with a too-hoppy brew and basket of snap peas.

* * *

Pavone kneels, hunches over her effects gear and slowly, gently, fades out, giving the piece a soft landing. Before a hush can settle she's tapping her bow on the strings, bouncing, dribbling. Piercing sounds zip across the room. No attack, no decay, just the piercing synth-like sound of pure peak. It's the Morse code rhythm that sticks. She drops the bow, slaps her palms on the strings, and the feedback roars on.

"Thanks, I'm Jessica Pavone. Pretty Monsters are up next." After kicking our collective can with immeasurable heaps of noise, stepping on our throats and swiping our wallets for good measure, it's the most concise of endings.

* * *

No signs of the usual crowd. Mark, the bartender, has the night off. James is absent, too. I'm used to seeing him up front, hugging half of the people who come in, doubling over in joy and disbelief as the music unfolds. It feels strange, like the hosts of the party are missing and there's a diplomatic vacuum. I feel a sense of obligation but don't know how to act on it.

Two stools to my left I notice a familiar-looking man, older, agitated. He says to no one and everyone: "Did you *hear* that? You didn't miss anything." He's referring to Pavone's set. The music has pissed him off and yet he stays. He didn't pay to get in, there's no cover charge, and he doesn't seem to be hanging out with anyone. He reminds me of Walter from *The Big Lebowski*, looking for support with full throttle belly aching. (*Am I wrong, Dude?*) He notices that Pavone is within earshot and backpedals. "It's not for everyone."

True, Walter, but that's why I come here, to hear something I've never heard before and won't hear again, something one-time and worth talking about. Isn't that why we're here? Comments like Walter's aren't the norm at Quinn's. I assume they happen, that many of these shows spark at least one heavy duty dose of "What was *that*?"—more judgment than astonishment—but this is the first that I've heard.

A younger man, mid-thirties, long-haired and bearded, takes the seat between Walter and me. He chats with Walter, puts Pavone's performance in context, makes peace, plays the Dude to the cranky one's Walter. (*No, Walter, you're not wrong. You're just an asshole.*) This is where archetypes come in.

* * *

I'm also a hybrid-driving public school teacher and card-carrying union member who's recently cut meat and dairy out of his diet, partly because my cholesterol is running high and partly due to ethical concerns. Stereotypes? I'm a *Star Trek* box set away from completing the picture. Or maybe it's time to check out *Dr. Who*.

* * *

If I'm surrounded by Walter and the Dude who does that make me? Donny, always asking questions and sharing observations that fall on deaf ears? The Stranger, the objective observer? Bits of both? Smokey?

* * *

Walter's fingers are knuckle deep in his ears when Katherine Young's Pretty Monsters come to life. (*This aggression will not stand!*) Young bombs the room with bassoon blasts. She's joined by Erica Dicker on violin, Owen Stewart-Robertson on guitar, and Mike Pride on drums.

I'm ready for more. Walter is not. He gripes. I look away. I don't want to take the bait. (Where do I recognize him from?) I notice the table behind me. Walter has unknowing allies. Twenty-somethings out for drinks, talking over the music. Pretty common stuff at Quinn's but the talkative types usually sit at the back tables. The Dude leans over and says that this particular group talked throughout Jessica Pavone's set, too. He's surprised that I hadn't noticed. Bubble-headed and unaware, they're like a bunch of Bunny Lebowskis. And the Nihilists, they have some of those louts in them, too—tossing marmots into the bathtub of an otherwise satisfying experience.

The avalanche that is Pretty Monsters soon buries Bunny and the Nihilists, along with the rest of us. Drums and shards of guitar, violin up high, bassoon down low. I see sheet music on stands and watch the band's eyes but can't tell when they're reading and when they're improvising. Their sound is wide and high and pushes aside anything in its way. The other players dash in and out, spokes around Young's eerie, leviathan tones. It's a fascinating choice of sonic center points, so many moments of startling contrast. Yet at other times I can't tell bassoon from violin from guitar.

There's ample open territory in their sound, places for single instruments, quiet to offset the noise. Or rather points at which quiet is intended. Instead it's stained by the yammering of Bunny and Nihilists, whose conversations I can't tune out.

Later I see Jessica Pavone and apologize for the sparse, distracting crowd. She shrugs it off, says it's a Monday night at a bar. True, but Quinn's is capable of better and I'm disappointed that that's not evident. I feel responsible, like such treatment could have been avoided if the regulars were on duty.

Walter stands and covers his ears. He turns away, glances toward the back entrance. I can't tell what he's looking for. There's no one blocking his way nor is the cavalry coming. Then, just as Mike Pride breaks into a solo, I realize that Walter is Ronnie, whom I met at the Accortet show, the guy who'd been buying yardsale instruments and resumed playing music. Walter/Ronnie calls out, "Finally, something that makes sense!"

The band plays on, unfazed. They've weathered worse. Later Erica Dicker tells me about playing at the International Jazz Festival in Gdansk, Poland with Anthony Braxton, Sally Norris, and Katherine Young.

"The audience was clearly expecting a black, American man to play them some nice 'sweating-brow,' straight JAZZ. They definitely weren't expecting a 'jazz master' and three white girls to sit down in chairs in front of music stands and play avant garde music. The reception was cold. People were engaging in conversation and speaking loudly during our performance. Others left the theater. I don't think there were any boos but I was amped up on adrenaline and remember leaving the stage feeling like I'd been punched in the gut—the vibrations in the space were very negative. The vibe in Gdansk was also negative. Even though we were in a more affluent area, clearly designed to accommodate tourist traffic, the icy, threatening looks Anthony received made Sally, Katherine, and I very uncomfortable."

The atmosphere was creepy, unsettling. She says that experience in Gdansk was a "nine or ten." She rates tonight a four.

Pretty Monsters thunder on, taking turns in the spotlight. I'm waiting for them to sandblast the room, clear the place. But they've set a different course, heavy and cacophonous, yet hinged and methodical.

Between songs the Dude turns and flashes a look of, Whoa, this is *out there*! "I wouldn't want to live where they live mentally," he jokes.

Dicker opens the next piece. Young looks down, nods, turns her head side to side. She seems to sense the template, perceives entry points. I don't have that level of focus. I can't keep the sounds of Bunny and the Nihilists from seeping in. I look over. So does the Dude. No use. They have their own agenda. (*We want the money, Lebowski.*)

Then Stewart-Robertson and Dicker change lanes, pour out tuneful, easy to discern lines that intertwine. Pride breaks out a xylophone, Young's bassoon bubbles up and the pieces melt together into something of a pop song. Ironically, with the band at its most accessible, Bunny and the Nihilists finally leave.

The next piece is mournful, reflective. In another time and place perhaps suited for looking back, a funeral or memorial. But the loudmouths have left and the tone is celebratory. Walter/Ronnie is still here but he's quieter. Pretty Monsters brought their avant chamber assault to the hinterlands and plunged their flag into the turf, fending off the naysayer and the ninnies. I'm annoyed by the band's reception, but they shrug it off—it's just strikes and gutters—and order drinks.

Mary Halvorson & Ches Smith | **Steve Ventura**

The Sun Is Shining, The Sky Is Boundless
Mary Halvorson & Ches Smith

"No more guitar heroes!"
—The Clash, "Complete Control"

The pine tree outside our dining room window is being cut down today. Last winter its branches—sagging with snow and ice—started snapping off and plummeting, falling fifty or sixty feet and spearing the ground. My son and I are glued to the window when the tree cutters arrive, watching the crew chief's ascent and the fall of the first broomstick branches. As he scales skyward the chainsaw clipped to his belt—slowly swaying, motor idling—hangs a few feet below his boots. He digs his ankle spikes into the bark and pushes higher.

* * *

Ches Smith's equipment forms a semi-circle. The drums face stage right, electronics straight ahead, vibraphone stage left. A cross-section of the inner sanctum, like a Jack Kirby diagram of the Baxter Building, or those scenes in Wes Anderson's *The Life Aquatic with Steve Zissou* that show a cut away of Zissou's ship, the Belafonte.

Smith concocts snare/bass combinations that pulverize, and the way he favors syncopation over speed allows you to savor each pop and punch. When he rotates to the synth/iPad, he plays with one stick, momentarily holds the other in his armpit, before switching to mallets, digs into increasingly abstract rhythms, climbs upward.

* * *

The larger branches have dinner plate diameters. The crew chief ties them off and lowers them to the ground. The other crew members guide the branches to graceful landings. The sky opens up, shades of blue replacing browns and greens. The ground is illuminated by direct sunlight for the first time in decades and even from our vantage point in the living room it feels warmer. The crew chief ascends to the top of the tree, reaches up and slices into the trunk, the very structure that's keeping him aloft. The falling pieces grow larger, the thumps louder, the sunlight brighter.

* * *

Smith rolls on his snare and discharges the synthesizer before turning to the vibraphone. He runs tests and gathers results, takes stutter steps before unleashing full runs. He starts a rhythm, repeats and alters it, plays along with one looped rhythm, then two. Smith forges ahead and tears down traditions, cuts into the structures he's leaned on.

Seeing him move from one instrument to another is like watching Steve Zissou aboard the Belafonte, on a quest to find the jaguar shark, going from station to station, checking on the sauna and the lab, up to the library, and down to the editing room. Like Zissou, Smith has devised an intricate system, fueled by the unpredictable, in the relentless course of running down, engaging with, and releasing something bigger than himself.

* * *

In the late '80s my cousin was stationed in the navy in San Diego. Near the end of his hitch he needed to get his car back to Syracuse but only had a few days. I flew out with his brother and the three of us drove back across the country, sprinted west to east in just under seventy hours. We spent a day at Mission Beach and then drove through the night, arriving at the Grand Canyon just before dawn.

* * *

Mary Halvorson shimmies from side to side, rocks back and forth behind a hollow body guitar. Her glasses slip to the tip of her nose as she dips and dives, rises and rolls across the covers from her solo debut album, *Meltframe.* There's something enchanting yet barbed in the tones she summons. Her songs emit a surprising intimacy given their labyrinth paths. Full steam ahead before skidding to a stop, smearing the sound, momentarily reversing course before resuming forward motion, like a DJ scratching a record.

* * *

The park was cloaked in darkness as we walked to the canyon. We wrapped ourselves in blankets and waited, chilly and bleary-eyed from the all-night drive, second-guessing the wisdom of spending so much time on a sight that remained hidden beneath the night's shadows. Then the expanse began to reveal itself. As first light trickled in we were struck by the depth, twenty, fifty, hundreds of feet down, no bottom in sight. Then we became aware of the width, yards then miles then lifetimes spanning farther and further. Then came the awe. The dimensions melted together, could no longer be considered in isolation. We were speechless before the splendor.

* * *

Halvorson's next piece opens with distress signal urgency, exhilarating fretboard dances that evolve into free form freakouts, on the precipice of being too much to ingest. Then she jump cuts, slows down and allows her tone to mushroom, wondrously large and enveloping. A rack of pint glasses rattles beneath the counter as Halvorson continues conjuring that Grand Canyon sunrise.

* * *

I assume Halvorson's set is the end of the show. She and Smith are on a "double solo" tour, traveling together but playing solo. Except tonight. While setting up earlier they overhear James and Steve, one of the co-owners, talking and realize the Quinn's contingent thinks that the guitarist and drummer will be performing as a duo. "There was a generous spirit in the house and they responded by doing a third set together," Steve later says. "Everything I've seen about their subsequent shows seems to indicate two solo sets and no more. We were privileged."

There's so much momentum from the previous sets that I foresee the duo show as bigger, more explosive, a relative summer popcorn blockbuster. Instead, Halvorson and Smith opt for a character-driven collaboration, like we're privy to a private dialogue. Across the room a woman shakes her head in disbelief while the man beside her closes his eyes and nods just behind the implied beat. The guy next to me has ordered a hot dog but doesn't eat until the set's over, waits for Halvorson and Smith to finish before taking a bite. We're mesmerized—staring, basking, monotasking. Our collective astonishment dilates as the music gradually expands, Halvorson and Smith breaking down and building up, fostering continuous cycles of depth, width, and awe.

Bathroom graffiti | Steve Ventura

Mary Halvorson, musician

I discovered this type of music gradually. If I had to trace it, I would trace it all the way back to Jimi Hendrix. He was my original inspiration for starting guitar at age eleven, though I can't remember how or why I was initially exposed to Hendrix. From there, I started taking lessons with a jazz guitarist, Issi Rosen, and started getting into jazz through him. Around the same time, I discovered my father's record collection, and began checking out Miles Davis, John Coltrane, and Thelonious Monk. None of this music was "love at first listen" and I didn't particularly like it or understand it at the time. However, the more I listened, the more I started to get drawn in, until I reached a point where I couldn't stop listening.

I remember listening to a Thelonious Monk compilation which was on a cassette tape/Walkman. I don't remember why I had the tape. It was probably my father's. I was on a hiking trip with my parents, and being probably twelve or thirteen, moody and in my own world, hiding in my headphones. I remember that during this hike I started to "understand" something about the music, enough so that I listened to the tape over and over and over again for most of the hike.

* * *

From there I branched out to Ornette Coleman and Charles Mingus. I discovered Wes Montgomery. Before I knew it I had somehow gotten to Derek Bailey by the end of high school. Then, when I went to Wesleyan University, Anthony Braxton was my professor, and through discovering his music I discovered a whole universe.

It felt like a momentary eye opening. I was thrown into [Braxton's] universe all at once, and was completely in awe of it all. It took me about a year to even begin to understand his language, the way he talked about music, the way his musical systems worked, and of course to be able to sight read and navigate some very difficult music. I remember reading excerpts from his Tri-Axium writings in my dorm, and spending hours outside of ensemble rehearsals trying to sight read the Ghost Trance music, and trying to decipher what it all meant. It was all very new and very exciting, but in this case I can say I was more or less hooked right from the beginning.

I remember learning about the AACM [Association for the Advancement of Creative Musicians], The Art Ensemble of Chicago, Joe Morris, Karlheinz Stockhausen, Sun Ra. At Wesleyan they had classes on Javanese Gamelan, African drumming, South Indian vocal music. I guess this is a long way of saying I started with Hendrix, fell in love with jazz and improvisation, and branched out from there.

* * *

I know a lot of musicians think about music visually, and are often inspired by still images, moving images, shapes, etc. My father is an architect, and I spent many years working administration in architecture firms. However, I don't normally think visually as I'm composing or performing music. My inspiration is usually more mood-related; trying to convey a particular feeling or an energy. If there *is* a visual element to the way I think about music, at least at this point, it's more unconscious.

* * *

One I remember specifically composing based on mood was the track "Spirit Splitter," the first track on the album *Away With You*. It was at the end of a particularly intense tour, and I was feeling pretty crazy and a lot of mixed emotions on the plane ride home. I felt the urge to compose and so I came up with the tenor saxophone melody and started writing the harmony parts on that plane ride. I think something about that song also evokes the feeling of being on an airplane. I try to not do it too often, and if I do, normally it's mindless work (fixing scores and so on), but occasionally I will put on headphones and try to actually compose something. Sometimes doing so in strange environments can be interesting.

Some of the others I don't remember the mood explicitly; or maybe I should say, it's hard to put it in words. But I enjoy composing when I'm feeling an intensity of emotion, mood, place; the music often flows out easier in those cases.

* * *

The project I'm focused on now is a quintet called Code Girl with Amirtha Kidambi, vocals, Ambrose Akinmusire, trumpet, Michael Formanek, bass, and Tomas Fujiwara, drums. I spent the last year writing lyrics—a very different creative process for me—and composing all the music. We recorded a double album that will likely be released next fall on Firehouse 12 Records. Aside from that, I don't have any specific plans other than trying to spend a bit more time at home so I can practice guitar and think about what I want to do next.

Truck Backs Up
Charlie Rauh
Jasmine Dreame Wagner

"Feeling loose on opening night
Steady nerves on opening night"
—The Figgs, "Opening Night"

My kids start summer vacation today. Maggie is next door at the neighbors. Sean is in the next room, lying on the couch, moaning.

"All I can do is lie here with my head over the garbage can," his groans exaggerated to signal his imminent demise.

He wants to watch television. Now his stomach hurts. He knows that being sick is often offset with tube time. I'm thinking "teach him how to fish." I tell him the story of the boy who cried wolf. This is not a moment that will make my parenting highlight reel but I figure there's a reason the thing has kicked around for centuries. He counters by saying he's never seen a wolf near our house. Score one for the boy.

In between his contrived coughs and continued pleas ("I'd feel better if I could watch *Clone Wars*!"), I try to recall a highlight from last night's show, something to serve as an intro, but the music was too sedate. It's like looking back on an afternoon of watching a river flow by and trying to recall a single moment, a specific drop of water.

* * *

Two days ago I came upon a near disaster when driving home, just after picking up the kids. I was about to cross the train tracks near our house when the car approaching me began to screech. It was a cherry red Celica and it sounded like the driver was slamming on the brakes. The front tires were smoking and yet the car kept moving forward. The front wheel was almost perpendicular to the body of the car. It was an unnatural angle, an automotive compound fracture.

When the car finally stopped, two guys, mid-twenties, slowly got out. They looked bewildered. I pulled alongside and explained what I saw: their axle was broken and sitting on the road. It must have snapped as they were driving along and dug into the pavement. They restarted the car and inched forward as far as they could. I thought they had cleared the train tracks. So did they.

A jeep pulled up behind the broken-down Celica. The jeep's driver was in a panic. He was the first to notice the Celica's back bumper was still above the rails. The car was stuck on the tracks.

Jeep dialed 911. "There's a 4:50 out of Patterson that'll be coming right over these tracks!" he announced, "You have to stop that train." My car's clock read 4:46.

* * *

Last night was opening night of a new weekly series at Quinn's. "Extreme Thursdays." Any other time and place I'd dismiss such a thing as a wannabe marking exec's stab at a metal or punk night. Probably sponsored by a hybrid sports drink/hot sauce startup. But it's Quinn's. I've seen so many extraordinary shows here. My hopes for the series are high. I missed the first six months of the Monday night series. I still hear about those early shows. But for this series I'm here on day one, opening night.

* * *

Chris Gethard, comedian: "These aren't opening nights per se, but every single time I perform standup for the first time at a new venue I get so nervous that I poop pretty much until the exact moment the host calls my name."

* * *

I drove ahead and parked on the side of the road. "No, daddy, you'll get hit by the train," my daughter said. Maggie is prone to panicking, but this is her way of saying be careful.

By the time I walked back to the tracks another car had arrived. The driver and passenger joined with the Celica dudes in nudging the car a few feet forward. The Celica was almost clear but we couldn't budge it any further. Jeep kept talking to 911. "The train will *certainly* hit the car. You must stop the train!" he pleaded.

The car wouldn't move and the train couldn't stop. The scenario was saturated with chaos, but there was order, too. Each individual exerted a small bit of control in a situation that had the potential to tidal wave us, toss everyone aside like corks.

* * *

Charlie Rauh opens the show. Solo guitar, all instrumentals. Very quiet. Very earnest. Very much the antithesis of extreme. And that's fine. I'm at a table with friends. Before and between songs we trade movie recommendations. Rauh's delicate tunes take me back through the day, walking west on Main Street, squinting in the setting sun as I crossed Fishkill Avenue. All those months of battling the cold and ice and snow, and now this, easing through days of seventy something perfection. It feels gluttonous.

Rauh's second song is even mellower, slower. The fake Christmas tree on stage, the one with the undulating lights, needs to be recalibrated. It's way ahead of Rauh's tempo.

My sense of ambient music is that it's about curbing disorder, pulling all parts under control, clearing the way for serenity. Ambient music doesn't speak to me but what does Rauh hear; what are his intentions? His music reminds me of driving home, late on a summer night, windows down, music off, totally spaced out and totally tuned in, solitary and peaceful. But I don't know how I could bring other people into such an experience.

* * *

Hallie Bulleit, dancer: "I don't think I have any rituals for opening nights. I normally find my rituals later into the run of a show. Then I get increasingly superstitious and habit-driven as time goes by."

* * *

John Ross Bowie, actor: "I have had very few opening nights. My ritual when I do *Big Bang* [*Theory*] is I have a Diet Coke and listen to Devo so as to get into my 'angry nerd' head. That helps."[3]

---

3 Bowie portrays Barry Kripke on *Big Bang Theory.*

* * *

I thought we should jack up the car, push it forward a few inches, and then repeat as needed until the Celica had cleared the tracks. The others agreed. Then a pick-up truck pulled up, window already down. "What the hell's the problem?" the driver yelled, "You've got to get that car out of the way!" We explained our plan. Truck ignored us. He had no time for deliberation. He turned over his shoulder and yelled at the car behind him. "Move it! Back up! Back up!" The window to his cab was closed. Truck yelled louder. The car moved.

Meanwhile Jeep was still talking to 911, the Celica's driver and his buddy were mumbling to themselves, my kids were waiting up the road in my car, and somewhere a train was rolling our way. Yet the pieces fit together, formed a functional whole. A resolution seemed to be within our grasp, though I'm not sure how much of that perception is hindsight and how much is denial.

Truck backed up, lurched forward, and shoved the Celica off the tracks. I thought he was going to roll down his window, verify that all was right, at least accept some gratitude. But that was not in his skill set. He gunned it and took off without saying a word.

That's when I saw the train coming around the bend. The gates dropped. We all stood back. The train rolled past and the Celica sat unscathed. Disaster averted.

* * *

Jasmine Dreame Wagner is up next. Solo keyboard and vocal. Very quiet. Very earnest. Very much in the vein of Charlie Rauh, though different. With quiet instrumentals my thoughts are fluid, my mind can wander. Once I hear lyrics, once there's language to account for, my field of view narrows, becomes binary. I'm more likely to think there's something to get, something to comprehend. Wagner's talent and tone match Rauh's but there's something I can't peg, something that anchors my thinking, prevents it from floating. Maybe it's the keyboard sound, which reminds me of Supertramp's inexplicably depressing *Breakfast in America*.

* * *

Chris Gethard: "Mostly at these clubs it's like, 'I hope I bring it, this could turn into a relationship where I get consistent work.' Being a comedian is odd because if a club likes me, they might put me up for like six to ten paying gigs a month. Every time you get that first shot at one, you're basically auditioning for a part-time job. And then there's also that dialogue of like 'I wonder how drunk the crowds get here, I'm new to this place.' I also tend to have some anxiety because I don't have a background as a club comedian, I come from the alt world. For me going into comedy clubs sometimes feels like I'm an emo guy going up at a hard rock club. Like they're not used to me. Club comedians are a little harder hitting and aggressive than I like to be. I guess the analogy would be that I sometimes feel like Elliott Smith playing at the Viper Room, and I'm just shitting and praying that it goes well and I can get them on my side."

* * *

I wonder to what extent Rauh and Wagner feel that Smith/Viper Room analogy? They must see the irony in bringing their soothing sounds to the opening night of Extreme Thursdays, such a different take on restraint/ release, what to keep in and what to let out.

* * *

My son flies into the room with a new Lego construction. His stomach ache is gone and he's running through the backstory for his latest design, barely able to keep up with his runaway thoughts, something about Batman flying a surfboard into Gryffindor. DC, Marvel, and J. K. Rowling all at once. His unbridled enthusiasm is streaked with mayhem and propels him through the day.

Jonas Bers' video synthesizer | Steve Ventura

Indoor Fireworks
Jonas Bers, Damian Cleary, & Matt Luczak

> "Walter, my old friend, where are you now?
> —The Kinks, "Do You Remember Walter?"

Hold tight. We're starting soon. James warns us the show will be loud. The staff has purchased extra ear plugs and anyone with photosensitive epilepsy may want to leave. People continue to trickle in. "Ignore my warnings at your own peril," he says.

* * *

Driving into Beacon clouds cling to hillsides, strands of cotton on velcro. A storm rides in, midnight black and ominous. Even ten miles out I can tell the clouds are coalescing over Beacon, targeting Quinn's. When the rain falls the wipers can't keep up and I count on the brake lights of strangers to find my way.

* * *

The lights go down. Extreme Thursdays: Opening Night, Part Two. I'm trepidatious, waiting to be deafened. Instead the band fades up, builds momentum in microscopic increments. Equally eerie and peaceful, like a quiet street at night. My mind is drawn to what might happen, what could occur.

Jonas Bers sits behind the video synthesizer. It's connected either directly or with contact mics to all of the other instruments—Damian Cleary's guitar, Matt Luczak's drum kit, and the rest of Bers' gear, synthesizer, steel guitar, and Walter, the PVC cello. "When Walter speaks," Bers says, "people stop."

* * *

I don't recall the weeks prior to Y2K that well, just vague recollections of mild panic and precautions, emergency rations and "What if..?" worries. The people I trusted most remained level-headed, which helped fend off nagging notions of paralyzed hospitals and airline catastrophes.

* * *

The video synthesizer produces waves in the kilohertz range, thousands of cycles per second. These are the vibrations we can hear. The synthesizer also produces waves in the megahertz range, millions of cycles per second. These are the vibrations we can see. The video synthesizer is wired to a projector which sits behind the counter, precariously perched atop the pie case turned beer cooler. The video synthesizer generates mounds of head-scratching sounds and streams of perplexing images.

* * *

Ironic that tonight's show is so tech-centric. I've been loathing all things twenty-first century, surfing a mile-high Luddite wave ever since my mp3 player deleted over forty-five minutes of an interview I'd recently recorded. I took every precaution I could think of. I checked and double-checked as the interview proceeded. I stopped the device periodically to keep the files reasonably sized. I played it back as I drove home. But when I attempted to upload the interview to my desktop, half of the files disappeared without a keystroke. I took the device to an expert. All he could do was apologize. I'd come so close to using a cassette and tape recorder, giving in to my old school tendencies. There's something about seeing wheels in motion, knowing that you can tinker, turn to the tactile, if things go awry.

* * *

I anticipated heavy synthesizer action paired with guitar and drums. I was prepared for a night of acoustic instruments vs. electronic instruments. Analog vs. digital. Monkeys vs. robots. But the group's gear is all analog, nothing digital, nothing binary. This includes the video synthesizer, which Bers built by gutting and rewiring an old keyboard ("the kind E.L.O. used"). Across the lower level he's changed out standard keys for dials, switches and protruding screws. Across the top he's added more screws, a field of them, like tiny mushrooms. He uses alligator clamps to make connections among the screws, always running the risk of receiving a shock. Wires sprawl this way and that. It looks primed for the climax of a Connery-era James Bond movie, snipping the right wire with seconds to spare.

Luczak moves to the snare drum, adding, raising, hovers but doesn't land. Cleary colors and shades, holds his guitar armpit high, thumps the instrument's body before turning it upside down, planting it on the stage and rotating it like a drill. Bers picks up a steel guitar repurposed from his grandfather's vaudeville days. They're busy like dinner-rush chefs but the notes are prolonged, lasting four or five seconds.

Meanwhile, the images are in hyperdrive, pouring across the backdrop, flashing for hundredths of a second. Black outlines on purple. A field of static. Colored squares. An ancient Hebrew text unearthed. The combined effect of sights and sounds is enthralling. I'd hoped for that. What I didn't anticipate was the sense of calm and control.

* * *

My wife and I spent New Year's Eve 2000 in St. Kitts, in the Caribbean, where she was going to school. Allie had heard there would be fireworks at midnight, so after dinner we found a spot halfway up a nearby hill. There were no other towns in the vicinity, no other islands in sight. The only lights visible in our world were those of cars twisting and winding along the country roads that ran through the fields of sugar cane.

* * *

More people enter between sets. When the music resumes Bers and Cleary get to the loud sooner while Luczak pushes the pace earlier. Three dudes walk in, glued to their glowboxes, oblivious to what's erupting on stage. Really, fellas? This is normal? Not enough to provoke a visible response?

There's a sudden squeal of feedback. Someone in back, someone beyond the blast zone, yells, "Ow, it hurts!" The sound person runs to the stage, assuming that something is wrong. But everything on stage is willful. Before the show Bers told me that sound people often don't know how loud the band wants to be. So when the music is quiet they turn up the volume, try to compensate, lend a hand. But that only eliminates the sonic head room, leaves nowhere to go. When the band turns up, everything "turns to mud."

* * *

Allie and I couldn't see or hear anyone else. We kept waiting for the fireworks or at least an outpouring of celebratory cheers to signify that

1/1/00 had arrived but the sky remained dark and the night remained still. It was several minutes past midnight before Allie checked her watch and we realized that Y2K had come and gone without fireworks, without so much as a flicker of lights. The next day we heard the fireworks hadn't started until nearly three in the morning because everyone was still in church.

* * *

The sound recedes. People clap. Maybe in appreciation. Maybe in relief. The applause elicits a grin from Luczak. *It ain't over yet, folks*. He goes double time on the kick drum, lights the next fuse. Cleary grinds away, producing ever more sound. Bers tinkers, moves alligator clamps from one screw to another. It might seem random but the looks of concentration say otherwise. It's like being inside the machine. Monkeys running the robot. I prepare for the trio to venture further out, launch what they've assembled. Instead they stay and investigate.

* * *

Spectres of the Spectrum mixes original and found footage, a dizzying array of clips from industrial and educational films, Kinescopes, ads, live action narratives, and animated shorts. In the film's commentary, director Craig Baldwin talks about "opening up material and discovering some secret within, coming upon ideas within this material left in the record, so to speak, and then spinning off of that."

* * *

Bers shifts the video synthesizer into full gear. Long, narrow, horizontal rectangles flash. Rainbow test patterns splatter. Checkerboards and sun beams. Atari graphics circa '79 and seventh-generation VHS dubs. A spontaneous collage of recent media history, secrets suggested within the flotsam and jetsam of progress.

* * *

On the one hand, *Spectres* tells the story of BooBoo and her father, Yogi, battling the New Electromagnetic Order. On the other, it's a compressed history of twentieth century America. Thinking of *Spectres* in this way sets up an inadvertent mental cage match: *Spectres of the Spectrum* vs. another example of "history of the century" media, Billy Joel's "We Didn't Start the Fire." Baldwin's messy, complicated greys versus Joel's straight up, black and white *It's not our fault!* concision. Analog vs. digital in a different guise.

And then Walter, the PVC cello, finally lumbers across the landscape. Bass pick-ups and strings stretched along four feet of pipe. Bers sits and reaches for a bow. Walter booms, rattles the joint, clears the way for decisive monkey victory as the band follows in his wake.

Joe McPhee | Michael Bogdanffy-Kriegh

In Lieu of Flowers
Joe McPhee & Chris Corsano

My day begins bedside. Persuading my mom, recently hospitalized yet still tenacious beyond measure, that it's time to leave her home of nearly fifty years and move out of her castle.

My night ends ringside. Watching two Quinn's mainstays, James and Steve, promoter and co-owner, argue about poetry long after the show is over.

"Olson doesn't need footnotes! Charles Olson is the greatest American poet!"

"What about Eliot? What about Ezra Pound?"

The day is dense with things that matter, as any day is, but today there's a more pronounced chasm between the realistic and the idealistic, what is and what should be. There is also the Joe McPhee/Chris Corsano show, two sets, each fantastic, each something everyone here can agree on.

* * *

From *SCTV*, Season One. A round table of film critics gathers for dinner. Host "Heraldo" Rivera, played by Joe Flaherty, attempts to moderate a discussion. Everything he mentions, cinematic or otherwise, is met with a chorus of contempt.

Heraldo Rivera: "One thing we can all agree on is the food here at Sardi's." Pauline Kael (Andrea Martin): "I haven't had a good meal since the '40s."

* * *

"We are only so lucky to be alive to disagree." —Matthew Specktor, *American Dream Machine*

* * *

Joe McPhee, saxophone, slowly ramps up, confident but not detached, sounds of every size and shape and hue emanate from the golden bell of his horn. Sounds high and loud and piercing, pitches that we're programmed to flee from in other settings. Sounds that signal, to many, *Get out of the way!* Sounds that beckon the fortunate to climb aboard, treasure the ride.

One of McPhee's instrument cases has a sticker that boasts: "Pissing Off the Planet…One Person at a Time." The case sits on the edge of the stage, up front and just off center.

Drummer Chris Corsano is McPhee's partner. His snare drum is tilted up, toward his hi-hat and crash cymbals, forming a percussive half pipe. Corsano lowers his left hand and rattles off a one-handed roll, see sawing on the rim of the snare. It doesn't seem possible, like a skater attempting a one-legged, 180 ollie.

* * *

After the show "What'd I Say" comes over the PA. The song's bridge alone, all the moans and groans, condenses the middle school health curriculum.

* * *

Whether taking giant steps or small strides McPhee saturates the senses with sounds that howl and coo, never bark, and when they bite it's with purpose. At one point he sings into his instrument, his voice ever so faint beneath the squeaks and squawks, struggling to be heard. Then he snips the safety line and sails off the tracks, brisk and loud. It's a sonic roller coaster less the long lines and rodent mascots and in-your-mug merch pushes. What better way to spend a summer night?

James tells the story of the time McPhee gave one of his albums to a neighbor. The neighbor wasn't familiar with McPhee's music, nor his reputation. He'd heard that McPhee had recorded, might be more than a weekend dabbler. McPhee ran into the neighbor a few days later. The neighbor's response: "People pay you to play like that?"

* * *

Corsano is set up on stage left. He's difficult to see from the back. People gravitate closer to get a better look. His snare is tilted the other way, slanted toward the floor tom. That's unusual, to see a drummer drastically change the angle of his snare. Did the stand slip?

* * *

I didn't take many of my mom's albums. She kept them tucked away in the hall closet, unplayed for years. Mostly Disney records from childhood and folk records from college. Nothing that I read about in record guides or those "Best Albums of All-Time" lists that I used to binge on in *Rolling Stone*. I swiped her copy of *What'd I Say* by Ray Charles, though. Housed in that heavy card stock of the era, the disc spilled out of the sleeve the first time I pulled it down. The title track sizzled my mind. The rhythms were just beyond my reach, something I could tap on a tabletop but not play on a drum kit, parts that I could sense more than replicate. And then there were the lyrics and his delivery. I can't picture my mom, whose other records were Jiminy Cricket and Kingston Trio, digging this.

* * *

A couple of McPhee's longtime friends are sitting next to me. One says to the other, "That was up the road." To which the other responds, "That was *way* up the road."

* * *

Something about McPhee's range and his willingness to steer away from the straight and narrow reminds me of Sarah Silverman. A few years ago Fox Sports invited her into the booth for an inning of a Red Sox/Yankees game. They paired her with Joe Buck, a smug, "hair trumps substance" broadcaster. She is funny and charming. She could tone down her act, vie for sitcoms and soda ads, but she tends to subvert. Presumably Fox knew this. Within moments she was totally inappropriate. She talked about "Massholes." She mentioned Doc Ellis throwing a no-hitter while on LSD, and joked that more pitchers should take acid before games. Buck wigged out. "No, we do not condone that whatsoever. No. No. We're going to the next topic." I would have too. I'm a parent, a teacher, a square when it comes to drugs. But I also know better than to give Sarah Silverman an open mic on a nationally televised game after she's confessed to barely following baseball and repeatedly admitting that she's "got nothing."

* * *

McPhee and Corsano interject references to other songs into their tunes, Thelonious Monk here, "Lift Every Voice," the African-American national anthem, there. They don't speak much between songs, just take a couple of breaths. Not the deep renewing breaths I expect, that I need mentally. Theirs is the breathing of conversation, gathering thoughts. Then one of them counts off—McPhee tapping his horn or Corsano a drum—and they're back on it.

When McPhee is asked about that sticker on his case he relates the story about his neighbor but ends the anecdote with a different line: "They pay you to play that shit?"

* * *

My mom was in her late thirties when she was diagnosed with rheumatoid arthritis. She never spoke of it. Never complained. Never wallowed. She never drew attention to herself, perhaps to a fault. Weeks would pass without any signs. But sometimes my brothers and I would hear her in the night, her knees, later her wrists and fingers, causing her so much agony, and all she could do was wait for the pain to pass. That was twenty-five, thirty years ago when I last lived at home. I can't imagine what she endures now. If we ask, then as now, she deflects, downplays what's she's going through, asks how we're doing.

* * *

Corsano's snare stand is wobbling now, a moving target. Then it tilts at an awkward angle, forty-five degrees, then sixty, but he's unfazed. He holds a stick with thumb and pointer finger, his other fingers splayed open, and surges on, using the stick then his palm to play the snare. Later I ask about his battle with the broken stand. "Let's just say it wasn't my intention," he jokes. "I'm just trying to listen to Joe." When the parts won't work like he wants them to, he puts others first and plays on. It's my mom's struggle in microcosm.

* * *

While visiting with family in Gloucester recently an uncle and I started talking about music. These nights at Quinn's came up, to which he said, "Jazz, oh, you mean the music that doesn't go anywhere." In hindsight, in some cases, I see his point, but it's not always about the distance traversed. In some ways McPhee and Corsano stay put on their final tune of the night. McPhee's face reveals great exertion yet his sound is so subdued, so quiet. Meanwhile, Corsano has brokered a truce with the troublesome stand. He's also reconfigured his snare drum with a banjo bridge and a cello string, his left hand pressing on the string, his right frantically sliding side to side. They match each other's pitches, the symbiotic nature of their relationship never more evident.

* * *

The show ends far too soon. Everyone is revitalized, chatty. But it's like a forest floor in mid-summer, dry, ready to be torched. I mention my trip to Gloucester. James asks if I'm familiar with the poet Charles Olson, who often wrote about the area. He nearly crumbles upon hearing that I'm unfamiliar with Olson's *The Maximus Poems*. Steve chimes in, sides with Ezra Pound, and it's on: *The Maximus Poems* vs. *Cantos*. I know neither, rarely read poetry. The fun is in the sparring, watching them reach for details, give high stakes treatment to things few reckon with. There's talk of a rematch on Steve's birthday.

* * *

"I nodded. I didn't disagree, but my friend had a right, just like me, to his own version of the tale." —Matthew Specktor, *American Dream Machine*

* * *

My mom concedes, admits it's time to move out, move on. Or maybe she's just appeasing me. It's not a debate I want to win. It may be the right choice but it feels wrong.

I ask her about the Ray Charles album. "What, you can't picture your mother listening to that song? That was good music when I was in college. We used to sing that at fraternity parties. I may have gotten that from your aunt. I think we used to do 'The Twist' to that one."

Now I know from whom she got the album and where and when and how she listened to it, danced to it even, but I still can't picture it. Later my brother tells me that she waited tables at a go-go club in the sixties.

* * *

"An American is a complex of occasions." —Charles Olson, "Maximus to Gloucester, Letter 27 [withheld]"

Joe McPhee and Steve Ventura | Michael Bogdanffy-Kriegh

Steve Ventura, Quinn's co-owner

I got into Frank Zappa at a very early age, like seventh grade, his first records were coming out. I lived in this little town called Raynham [Mass.] that was next door to Taunton, which was bigger, fifty thousand people. The first and only head shop, ever in Taunton, was called The In Thing. This was late '60, early '70s. They had a little record bin and it was a funny place. It was a funny time. The owners, when you were walking by the store you could look in and see they'd just be sitting there smoking joints. [laughs] It's like, is this illegal? Doesn't seem it. I used to go there for records. One of the records I bought there right after it came out was Zappa's *Weasels Ripped My Flesh.*

That record had a song titled, "The Eric Dolphy Memorial BBQ." So I was going through the bin at The In Thing and they had an Eric Dolphy record, *Out to Lunch*. Eric Dolphy is such a perfect person to start you on that path. Dolphy played with Mingus. He played with Coltrane, Bobby Hutcherson, Mal Waldron, Booker Little. If you're stretching out and finding different records Eric Dolphy is on, you're going to end up with a lot of really great jazz records. I remember the second jazz record I ever bought was a Yusef Lateef record, *Psychicemotus*. The third one was probably a Mingus record. *Oh Yeah*, I think. I still listen to all these records. Forty-five, -six years later.

I met Frank Zappa in high school. My sophomore English teacher was Ms. Underwood. There was an older guy who sold pot and stuff in Taunton who I knew casually. He ended up living with this teacher. Like I said, the times were really different. [laughs] I used to go over there in the mornings, drink coffee and whatever. One of these mornings I said, "Are you any relation to Ian Underwood?" I expected her to say, "Who's that?" And she said, "Oh, the guy who plays reeds with Zappa? Yeah, he's my first cousin, I grew up in the house next door to him." [laughs] That was a big shock. She calls her cousin and we ended up going to the sound check, which was amazing. At the time, I drew a lot of pictures of Frank Zappa to put on my bedroom walls. [laughs] It was like a Christian meeting Jesus or something. We went to the sound check and then we went out to supper with Frank and Gail Zappa and Ian and Ruth Underwood. I didn't talk a lot. I was in complete awe. At one point, Frank said to me, "So where you from?" I said, "Raynham." He said, "Oh, they have a dog track." [laughs] He knew that somehow. [laughs] They were nice to me. The show that night was Captain Beefheart, Alice Cooper, and Frank Zappa. That was quite an experience. Thank you, Ms. Underwood! [laughs]

Once I got my license I would drive into Boston and go to the Jazz Workshop and Paul's Mall. Nobody stopped you from going into bars. I had a beard when I was really young, so that helped. I got to see Mingus in the early '70s. I drank the first bourbon of my life because I saw Mingus order one during the break. I saw Sun Ra at least a dozen times. Jonathan Swift's was a place in Cambridge where I saw the Chicago Art Ensemble and so much else. Great place, long gone.

Zappa also quoted Iannis Xenakis, so I got into twentieth century classical experimental music. Who was the other guy that he was always quoting—"The present day composer refuses to die"? Edgard Varèse. He did a symphony for sirens. That opened that worm hole, and I got sucked in and never left. There were long periods of my life where I didn't listen to anything with a melody or a repeating pattern of beats.

I was also a crazy record collector. I would buy things without knowing what they were if they were on a label that I'd gotten other good things on. FMP, Intakt, Arc, Hat Hut, Po, on and on. I ended up with all this small label European stuff. Who's that trumpet player from Poland? Tomasz Stańko. Fantastic records, that early stuff of his. Peter Brötzmann and Evan Parker. The chase—it's hard to find this stuff, there was no internet back then. [laughs] The first time I went to Canada was to go to a record store. [laughs] The only time I've ever been in Princeton, N.J. was Princeton Record Exchange. There was a store in Philadelphia where, I had gotten a Christmas bonus, I spent like eleven hundred dollars on jazz records. I had two clerks help me get to the car. [laughs] I remember one six-month period I listened to nothing but Cecil Taylor, because I had like thirty Cecil Taylor records I had never heard. [laughs] Once you've seen Cecil Taylor, you're either going to leave or you're there forever.

In the early '90s I was doing music for experimental theatre at a place called Perishable Theatre that was attached to AS220, which was the center of experimental music and theatre and everything else in Providence. Still going strong. I first saw Jack Wright there. There was a thing every month called The Cabaret of the Oddly Normal. Weird performance artists. I did my Church of Frivolity shows there; a play with no words. I did *Hamlet* in ten minutes, every single word from *Hamlet* in ten minutes. I had like thirty-five people all reading at the same time. [laughs] And then when it came time for Hamlet to get stabbed in the sword fight, everybody died and knocked over everybody's table in the place. [laughs] The guy who ran the place was one of the readers and he was the first one to knock over a table. [laughs] He was great. Bert Crenca. He was the center of experimental stuff in Providence. He's the grandfather of it. Still going. He's a painter primarily, but he had bands. He turned me on to great writers. He was and is amazing.

My wife, Sue, and I were thinking of moving to Brattleboro, VT, but we ended up coming to Beacon and really liking it. Then Tom, an old college friend, and his wife Yukie [Schmitz, Quinn's co-owners] were living in Beacon and going off to Japan for two or three weeks. Sue got two weeks off, so we lived in their house and explored. First night I was here I went to Dogwood [bar and restaurant located near Quinn's] and ended up sitting next to James Keepnews and talking jazz. I knew the European stuff and he knew absolutely everything there was to know about the New York scene. That is where the story starts: me meeting James Keepnews, who's indispensable to what we are. His signature is all over the place. As soon as we start talking about Quinn's, we started talking about jazz at Quinn's. James said, "Well, who would you want to get?" The very first name I said was William Parker. The very first show we had was William Parker. The second name I said was Tani Tabbal. That was the second show.

James knew everybody, could get in touch with everybody. Now I'm booking stuff, too, but it's mostly because of all these connections that had been made through James. I was calling Joe McPhee the other day. I never saw that coming. I never thought I'd call Iva Bittová and have her give me Fred Firth's number. [laughs] I've been so into these people for so long. They're the nicest people in the world. I think that both free jazz and punk can be very freeing forms of expression. I think that's why the people who do it tend to be really nice and easy to get along with. They get all that shit out of them. [laughs] They have another means to get it out. Their vocation is to transcend the bullshit.

One of my greatest joys is bringing young musicians in. Steven Frieder. Fan*tas*tic band. Adam Siegel is another. Absolutely amazing. I met him because of Tani Tabbal. Tani Tabbal brought him down from Woodstock. There's this whole thing and I feel like I'm part of it now. It's an immense privilege.

Distant Thunder, Local Thunder
Man Forever
Mike Gamble

"On lucky nights I dream that I can fly"
—Kelly Hogan, "Lucky Nights"

Despite my allegiance to shows at Quinn's, I need some bait on the hook before I decide to go. Weeknight shows involve a bit of juggling on the home front and I want some sense of what awaits, the prospect of a worthy adventure. I looked up Man Forever online but what I found generated more questions than it answered.

I wasn't able to find anything on the opener, Mike Gamble, a one-person band—guitar, drums, and laptop. He's wearing a white dinner jacket and a multi-colored "Won it at the state fair" hat. Combined with his leopard print guitar strap, I'm left unsure of where he's headed. Van Halen in a funhouse mirror? Harmony Korine-caliber cringing?

* * *

"Fielding Melish, the president of San Marcos, goes on trial tomorrow for fraud, inciting to riot, conspiracy to overthrow the government, and using the word 'thighs' in mixed company." —Woody Allen, *Bananas*

* * *

Gamble sits behind a snare drum and floor tom, playing guitar, a laptop to his left. His guitar parts are melodic, surfy at times, yet slowed down and expanded. Feedback lurks but doesn't puncture as he slaloms between intense strumming and tender flourishes—push, push, coast. Then he plays back a portion of the guitar track and finds a beat, accompanies his moments-ago self on drums, time traveling back to the conversation he's just initiated.

So much music is about linear progress, the passage of time, verse into chorus. A followed by B. Gamble's method is more spatial, verse *and* chorus, A on top of B. The audience is able to make more decisions, find bits we overlooked the first time amid the one-person call and response.

* * *

Fielding Melish, played by Woody Allen, acts as his own attorney. He poses questions, leaps into the witness stand to respond, then returns to the courtroom floor for further questioning.

Fielding Melish, lawyer: "I would not joke with this court if I were you."

Fielding Melish, witness: "*Wouldn't* you or *couldn't* you?"

Fielding Melish, lawyer: "Does the code name Sapphire mean anything to you?"

* * *

I've not heard of Man Forever, so I go online. I find footage of the Man, drummer Kid Millions, aka John Colpitts, playing drums in a variety of mobile settings. He performs in rush-hour subway cars and aboard an airplane. He plays in a shipping container. ("One of the biggest

nightmares of my performance career. I really didn't think it through...
How was I going to get a steady flow of oxygen into the container?")
There's also a clip where he sits in the back seat of a luxury sedan and
rolls on his snare drum while a friend drives. ("Most people were saying
my career was more or less dead.")

Kid Millions doesn't go out of his way to show off his chops. It's just
him and a snare—his location eclipses his performance, which only
makes his goals more ambiguous and the pieces more enticing. A
strange mix of Keith Moon and Andy Kaufman? How much winking is
involved? I relish the uncertainty, sifting through the possibilities and
drafting theories.

* * *

"Andy Kaufman went way beyond blurring the distinction between
performer and persona, past the point where you wondered what
separated the actor from the character; you wondered if he himself knew
anymore where the boundaries were drawn. What did he get out of such
performances? The joy of not telling the audience how to react, giving
that decision—or maybe just the illusion of such decision making—back
to the audience." —David Shields, *Reality Hunger*, quote #490[4]

4 When I read that passage in *Reality Hunger* I thought, Yes, exactly! I wish I'd said that.
Then I realized that I had. I recalled an email exchange I had with Shields prior to the book's
publication:

> I'm working on a new book called *Reality Hunger: A Manifesto*, in which I'll be
> attempting to articulate my aesthetic. Below is a brief riff I've written on Andy
> Kaufman. What would you want to add to this if anything?"
>
> Thanks for any thoughts.
> David
>
> "Andy Kaufman used to do a bit in which he was a character playing a character
> playing a character. There was no 'real Andy Kaufman.' You could never quite
> touch ground. You never felt safe."

* * *

Kid Millions: "We're going to do one piece tonight. I think you'll be able to tell when it's over."

Left to right, Man Forever is Matt Evans, bongos, Kid Millions, full kit, Max Almario, snare drum. They're grouped together, U-shaped, clustered in the center of the stage. Their performance is pure joy, anti-prank. Yet, the sight of bongos reminds me of Andy Kaufman, who often played congas onstage. Combined with the videos of Kid Millions, part of me is looking for a put on.

* * *

David,

Thanks for writing. This is one of my favorite topics, in part because I've never completely figured it/him out. I just watched Andy's ABC special and here's what is swirling through my mind.

Andy Kaufman goes beyond blurring the distinction between performer and persona, past the point where you wonder what separates the actor from the character and reaches that rare point where, for a moment, I wonder if he knows where the boundaries are drawn—there are flashes of being concerned for his mental health (Is it okay for a person to go that far out on the limb?). Then I wonder what he gets out of such a performance and I speculate that it's rooted in the joy of not telling the audience how to react, of giving that decision (or maybe just the illusion of such decision making) back to the audience, which is liberating for some audience members and, I imagine, disconcerting to others. Also, from what I've read, he often stayed in character backstage when among fellow performers, people who expected to receive the wink and a glimpse into the "real" Kaufman, and many of them resented being treated like an audience member, a civilian.

I don't know that that adds in any way to what you've already considered, but if I can be of any further help let me know.

Mike

In *Reality Hunger*, David Shields sculpts 618 quotes into a call to arms to "ignore the laws regarding appropriation, obliterate the distinctions between fiction and non-fiction, and create new forms for the twenty-first century." Some of the quotes are his, others are appropriated. None of the quotes are cited, though there are footnotes in the back of the book. According to the appendix, Random House lawyers determined the footnotes were necessary. "If you would like to restore [the] book to the form in which I intended it to be read," Shields notes, "simply grab a sharp pair of scissors or razorblade or box cutter and remove pages 210-218 by cutting along the dotted line." I had a hunch, purely speculative, the footnotes and talk of lawyers were a prank.

When Shields appeared on *The Colbert Report* to promote *Reality Hunger*, Steven Colbert cut out the notes and tossed aside the rest of the book.

* * *

Matt Evans steps toward and back from his bongos like a dance partner. Max Almario, motionless from the shoulders down, bobs his head, chicken pecks, as his snare cuts through the mix. Then there's Kid Millions, eyes closed, mouth open, working up a summer sweat. He plays with the enthusiasm of Max Fischer, Jason Schwartzman's character in *Rushmore,* but heightens his bright-eyed attitude, trades aspirations and approximations for experience, a performance both loftier and more grounded.

Millions opens the set with a barrage of eighth notes on the kick drum. The tempo won't change for the next half hour. Neither will the instrumentation. Just drums and piles of riveting rhythms, percolating patterns always and never changing, thundering like buffalo charging across the plains. The absence of breaks or pauses keeps us enveloped in their calling, surrounded and insulated. Man Forever are relentless.

* * *

Russian Ark is comprised of a single ninety-six-minute shot. There are no breaks in the film, no edits. One camera followed the action from set to set. It's an astounding level of commitment but I turned it off after ten minutes. I needed to blink. I needed those momentary breaks that come with changing camera angles.

* * *

David Shields: "I wish I'd thought of [the notes in *Reality Hunger*] as a mock-requirement that I'd planned all along. In fact, it was a begrudging compromise worked out with [the] publisher."

* * *

Man Forever storms ahead and we sit awestruck, as if in a wind tunnel, the old Maxell ad come to life, pints and T-shirts in place of wine glass and leather jacket. How can something so loud and varied be so trance inducing and unified? I can see each member of the band but it takes a moment to determine the point of origin, figure out who's making what. Eventually I change tactics, take in the whole rather than untangle the parts. Like birds in flight, they take their place one after another at the front of the flock, moving to the fore, then dropping back as the next takes his place. Darting ahead, falling back.

There's no Tubby Time to close shop tonight. The King abdicates in favor of A Tribe Called Quest and we talk, buzzed on great music, chasing down words to capture the experience, eager for more.

Dan Loomis | Michael Bogdanffy-Kriegh

Find Out What It Means
Josh Rutner Trio

"I don't get no respect."
—Rodney Dangerfield

I was Rodney-ed twice when I bought the latest Bob Mould record. The first from a clerk in her early twenties.

"Are you getting that? It's pretty good."

Her tone was patronizing, like SHE WAS SPEAKING TO ME VERY S-L-O-W-L-Y AND IN ALL CAPS, ADDRESSING A CONFUSED OLD MAN WHO'D SOILED HIS SHORTS AND WANTED TO PAY WITH GREEN STAMPS AND A SACK OF YAMS.

No surprise, right? A little condescension from a twenty-something watching a forty-something buy new music made by a fifty-something. I certainly thought worse things when I was in her position, working at a record store in the early '90s, every inch the judgmental know-it-all, watching some Woodstock casualty shell out for the new Crosby, Stills, and Nash album.

* * *

It's another perfect summer night—clear skies, "shorts or slacks?" temperatures, and just enough condensation on my pint glass to remind me that my snow shovel can keep collecting cobwebs. Young couples sit at the counter, older folks, too, sipping and flirting. Hipsters and geezers co-existing. It's a wonderful thing.

* * *

The second response came a moment later from a clerk in his mid-fifties, about ten years my senior.

He spied my pending purchase and coyly asked, "Do you remember?" His tone implied that, in fact, I did remember.

"Huh?"

He said it again, "Do you remember?"

"I'm not sure what you're talking about."

"Do you know his first band, Hüsker Dü?"

For years I frequented the record stores of downtown New York, forever leery of being subjected to the scorn of some mopey clerk who was judging me by the records I'd chosen. But nothing like that ever happened. Those clerks were many things—indifferent, distracted, hung over, hard of hearing, humorless—but never so obviously playing a status game. I found it amusing that now, buying the Bob Mould album at age forty-five, that I received a dismissive dose of "Hmm, not sure you're worthy of that record."

"Yeah, sure, I know Hüsker Dü," I said, still unsure of what he was driving at.

He hesitated, stared, gave me some patronizing wait time. His tone small font rather than all caps: *"Are you sure there isn't something you want to tell me? Come on now, this will be much, much easier if you say it. Come on now, think."* He let another moment pass before explaining that Hüsker Dü translated to "Do you remember?"

"Oh, right, I knew that."

He gave me the subtlest of "Sure you did" eye rolls.

Too old to hang with the hip and unworthy of the wise. If only I had a necktie to loosen.

* * *

Saxophonist Josh Rutner's sound has a jittery undertone, pleasing but unsettled, pursuing. Like Sonny Rollins, he has an excellent sense of when to go with a rhythm, play it tuneful and memorable, and when to give it some teeth.

* * *

Quinn's has a hipster element, sure—there's a flow of young Brooklyn expats, among others—but hipster-friendly never sinks to hipster doofus. The '50s style luncheonette décor is largely intact, kitschy but authentic. People are approachable and the prices are reasonable, which appeals across generations.

* * *

Rutner stays in bounds with his tone, but not always, not absolutely. He tackles the age-old challenge of working within the confines of a genre, adhering to the unwritten rules, while bending or breaking them to establish his voice.

* * *

Jason Turbow's *The Baseball Codes* looks at the many unwritten rules of the national pastime and the ways in which players get tangled up in the endless contradictions within those rules. My favorite being Ben Davis of the Padres bunting to break up an eighth inning no-hit bid by Curt Shilling of the Diamondbacks. Davis followed one rule—always play to win—but broke another—bunts ain't for busting up no-hitters. Davis incurred a heap of "*You don't do that!*" from old and new schoolers alike. The righteous indignation that followed, the red-faced anger was pervasive. *That's not how you respect the game.*

* * *

Bassist Dan Loomis and drummer Jon Wikan round out tonight's trio. The group takes a couple of tunes to find their footing. Loomis and Wikan exchange knowing glances and mischievous grins, glances and grins that go beyond the typical rhythm section having a good time. Are they challenging each other? Trying to trip each other up? Is Rutner aware of their dialogue?

* * *

Jason Turbow: "Because of a Google alert set to 'unwritten rules' I see stories all the time about the unwritten rules of office etiquette...and riding elevators...and Facebook...and etc. Ultimately, these things all boil down to respect, both of the people participating and of the process itself. How that gets defined is where the interest lies."

* * *

Maybe I'm reading too much into the non-verbal stage banter, looking for ways in which the band is adhering to or breaking protocol. Maybe it's all in-bounds. Maybe they're just animated performers. Loomis is talking to himself and his instrument, coaxing it along—*Come on, we got this*. Man and machine as one, the antithesis of David Herman's plight in *Office Space*, unleashing his aggression on the office fax machine. "C'mon, let's go! That's what I need! Let's do that! Let's do *exactly* that, you little…."

No respect at all.

* * *

Wikan is animated, too: his performance, his demeanor, his share of the knowing looks, even his loud button-up shirt. He stops and starts, changes beats, alters trajectories.

* * *

Jason Turbow: "There are certainly unwritten rules of jazz. When Oscar Peterson recorded the *Exclusively for My Friends* sessions in Germany, it was unspoken between him and Ray Brown that Brown would take the lead in ways that Ed Thigpen was not expecting, and that led to some very awkward tension."[5]

* * *

Dan Loomis: "So many looks for so many reasons."

* * *

---

5 Jason Turbow: "That would be way cool if I hadn't made it up."

Wikan reminds me of a '70s character actor, bit parts on *Barney Miller*, hauled into that ancient holding cell before the first commercial break, cracking wise with Fish and Yemana, antagonizing the rank and file while charming the audience.

* * *

Rutner is Barney Miller, the bemused leader, tolerating the hijinks while running the ship. Loomis is Wojo, the good-natured go between.

* * *

But enough of sitcoms. They aren't on my mind while the band is playing, not much anyway, certainly not by the third tune. The trio has an undeniable and irresistible cohesion. Think of all the ways people communicate these days—all the overpriced, high maintenance devices we cling to—and these three are duking it out with sticks and strings, chunks of metal and tubes.

This is when the looks of "They are *on* it" circulate. Rutner and Loomis lock into the refrain, loop it as Wikan goes off, unleashes what he's been hinting at, the perfect setup for Rutner's next passage, which is quiet, vulnerable. A raw nerve exposed.

Wikan opens the next number with a rack tom bounce that reminds me of "St. Thomas" by Sonny Rollins. Ironic that Rollins would come up again. Last week the *New Yorker* ran a piece titled "Sonny Rollins: In His Own Words." It purports to be an open letter from Rollins, but was written by Django Gold, an *Onion* contributor. The letter has Rollins regretting he devoted his life to music and generally disparaging jazz. The piece ticked off a lot of fans for a variety of reasons. Many focused on Gold's decision to present his satirical point of view as that of Rollins's voice and also, initially, the *New Yorker*'s decision to not run a disclaimer. *It's about respect. You don't do that.*

* * *

Chris Kelsey, musician: "If the music isn't big enough for us to shoo away a petty annoyance like this Gold bug, maybe it deserves to be the exclusive province of cultists that it's well on its way to being."

* * *

Vince Kueter, writer: "What if it's an Andy Kaufman-esque stunt and the over-reaction is the key part of the performance?"

* * *

Rodney Dangerfield: "Every time I get into an elevator the operator says the same thing, Basement?"

* * *

Josh Rutner: "That night was the first night I'd played with (and even met!) Jon. Any looks shot around the group were most likely approving, 'all right' looks."

* * *

I'm fascinated by the band's efforts to shape their sound. I wondered if there was some measure of discord in those looks, some break with "the right way," but there wasn't. And just to punctuate that that wasn't part of the proceedings, the show ended with Wikan's daughter, probably six or seven, scurrying this way and that, overjoyed, imbuing everything with the feel of a summer picnic that's run long into the night.

Peter Evans | Michael Bogdanffy-Kriegh

Communication Overdrive
Peter Evans & Sam Pluta

"If you put all the knobs on your amplifier on 10 you can get a much higher reaction to effort ratio…Just a tiny tap on the strings can rattle your windows, and when you slam the strings, with your amp on 10, you can strip the paint off the walls…and with a tiny movement rule the world."
—David Fair, from the liner notes to Half Japanese's *Greatest Hits*

Words have been failing me lately. This afternoon a co-worker called with an easy request. I was willing to comply. I was able to comply. But I couldn't communicate either of those facts. The more I tried to convey that all was well, that his request was reasonable and easy to fulfill and already half done, the more he felt the need to explain what he wanted and why, and the more agitated he became. The more I spoke, the worse it got.

* * *

The crickets are cranky when I get home after the show, unusually loud, rattled by something in the air. I credit Peter Evans and Sam Pluta. They've set something in motion that reverberates for miles and hours.

* * *

The more I try to support my mom and help her sort through her situation—needing neck surgery, having to find an apartment, and sell her home—the further we drift, the more she doubts my motives, and the more I add to her frustration. I haven't found the right words.

* * *

To some extent there's always a variance between expression and reception, some contrast between what we intend and what's understood, output and input. With Peter Evans (trumpet) and Sam Pluta (electronics) that contrast is intentional, the juxtaposition of their instruments, analog and digital, metal and plastic, is at the core of the design.

Peter Evans doesn't play trumpet so much as survive it. I'm surprised he walks away from the experience unscathed. He blows like a man living on borrowed time, as if he's thrown himself on a live grenade and has but a few moments to divulge a deep well of secrets—*You've* got *to hear this! And this! So much to say, so little time—and are you listening?*

Sam Pluta, meanwhile, sits at a table of electronics—iPad, Manta keypad, laptop. He performs with equal fervor, coordinating a million missions impossible, sampling Evans' trumpet lines, reshaping and regurgitating them. One moment a succession of piercing, shrill sixteenth notes. The next, table-rattling half notes that plunge to Mariana Trench depths. I glance over at the glass drink case behind the counter as if it might shatter.

* * *

I'm still stressed from work when I arrive at the show, frazzled by a long, taxing, head-spinning day of preparing for the start of school. I accomplished a lot Monday through Wednesday. Today, though, I went into my last meeting with three things on my "to do" list and left with a dozen.

* * *

Witnessing Evans shove so many ideas through his mouthpiece is like watching traffic funnel into the Holland Tunnel. But those cars crawl, mark their journeys a few feet at a time. Evans has six—or eight or twelve—lanes of ideas barreling ahead, accelerators stomped to floorboards, yet somehow converging.

Pluta bends to rhythms I can't hear and leans into the noise, uses body English like a bowler or a ballplayer, Carlton Fisk in game six. His every action carries purpose, even when he pushes up his glasses, one index finger on each bow, none of this "jab at the bridge" nonsense.

Watching them perform, seeing their sounds streak about the club reminds me of the lightbike races in *Tron*—the speed, the turn-on-a-dime joyride thrill of breaking from norms, one "illegal exit" after another.

* * *

Allie had to work late tonight. I wasn't sure that I'd be able to make the show, and with the nonsense from work I wasn't sure that I wanted to. I thought it might be best to go to bed early and start over tomorrow. James and Steve spot me when I arrive, treat me to a welcome dose of the "Norm entering Cheers" treatment. Eric passes along a copy of the Juice Glover book we've been talking about and he asks about my mom. Then Joe McPhee shows up, not to perform, but as a civilian, to watch and hang His presence prompts us to exchange "Did you see who's here?" looks and bask in the further validation of our budding scene. Each interaction sands down the workday residue, takes the edge off. I'm still not sure how much I'm ready to be challenged but that's comically irrelevant in light of what Evans and Pluta uncork.

* * *

Evans puts his hand to the trumpet's bell, pulls out the notes, clears the way with a magician's touch and a wrecking ball's impact. His motions can be gentle but the results pummel. Meanwhile, he's worked out a dance with the microphone. In one regard, he's restricted physically, tethered to the mic—he needs to keep supplying raw material for Pluta—but he turns that limitation, that friction, to his advantage. It's traction that drives him forward. The evident action is from his neck up, but like an active volcano there's much more bubbling below, alveoli working overtime.

Pluta utilizes a Manta keypad. It became his "main axe" about six years ago. Slightly larger than a clipboard and covered with a series of octagonal keys, it lights up with each touch, illuminating Pluta's fingertips, each tap adding to the unceasing rush. As for the laptop, with its countless overlapping windows, it's only for display. "If I looked at that I'd get distracted," he says.

* * *

When I teach it's imperative that words affect change. It's the essence of the gig. I'm used to delivering unwelcome information at times, even flat out failing to communicate, but I'm part of a dialogue in which language routinely, if imperfectly, moves things ahead. But no matter what I say I can't change things for my mom. For the longest time I thought the details were bogging me down—when she'd sell the house and where she'd go from there—but they're secondary. The hard part has been realizing that no matter what I say, no matter how carefully I select my phrasing, words cannot alleviate her physical challenges. They do nothing for her pain and frustration.

* * *

Evans and Pluta lean less on the features that typically draw me to music—melody, harmony, rhythm. Yet for all the noise it's the quiet, subtle acts that provide the tractor beam, the way they listen, give and take, react and communicate, soothe in surprising ways. I need a show like this, something that overpowers the baggage I bring to it, treats my headspace like taffy on a stretching machine, and reaffirms—at jet engine decibels—why we keep trying.

Iva Bitova | Michael Bogdanffy-Kriegh

Agree and Add
Iva Bittova

"Don't you know that it takes time?"
—Tenement, "Earwig"

The room is pin drop quiet, fully occupied and yet uncommonly still, entranced. Iva Bittova's performance projects a serious, high art vibe and we lock into concert hall reverence. But her stage presence, her persona, has a folk art vibe. She is well-versed at disarming our perceptions and projections, mine at least. She encourages people to sing and clap along. She scats and snaps her fingers. She welcomes the applause but wants a more active audience while the songs are underway. ("Are you okay? So quiet. Thanks for clapping.") She's funny, too, gently chiding us: "I was in China recently. The Chinese sing along easily." Polite but pointed Czech heckling.

* * *

I felt dizzy when I sat up last Wednesday morning. The exterior of my body felt normal, muscles contracting, head and shoulders slowly rising from the pillow. The interior, however, was stuck in a different gear. My brain languished behind, trailed by two or three miserable beats. There was a woozy separation between vision and understanding. I imagine that a photograph of that moment would resemble a double exposure.

* * *

Iva Bittova stomps on the stage, emphatically yet elegantly, punctuating the end of a song as waves of adulation crash the room. I lose sight of her as she steps down. She emerges a moment later, standing in the middle of the room, sipping tea, with a most beguiling look of confidence, gratitude, and beatification.

The Czech vocalist and violinist recognizes that her show could be construed as unconventional—challenging, uncompromising—yet she is still looking to connect. "Hopefully you'll not be surprised so badly," she says early on.

Her vocal range is dizzying. She soothes, then shrieks, zips through all manners of pitch and volume. Likewise for her violin performance, from lullaby to frenzy. Then she turns from the mic and gestures like a Theremin player, hands frolicking along the x- and y-axes of an electric field. The person next to me leans over to say, "Every time I think I have it figured out she changes the channel." I can relate, engaged throughout the show but uncertain, heart and mind out of step.

* * *

Wobbling across the bedroom I felt like I was at sea, being tossed and turned. I had to grab the bed and dresser to remain upright. The same thing happened the day before. I took a sick day and scheduled a doctor's appointment. He said that I had vertigo, that my internal gyroscope was out of sync. My body needed an extra moment to process incoming information. There was a disconnect between the external and the internal.

* * *

Most of Bittova's compositions have lyrics. I'm not used to thinking about language at these shows, the vast majority are all-instrumental. Some of Bittova's songs are in English, but most are "in some Czech and some in my own language." I can't tell the difference. The experience reminds me of watching comedians speak in gibberish, letting go of the language's literal meaning and allowing other factors to do the talking.

* * *

In Philip K. Dick's *A Scanner Darkly*, Fred, an "undercover narcotics cop," is spying on his alter ego, Bob Arctor. Over time, he loses the ability to distinguish between the two roles, one forgets that he's the other. The two sides of his personality come together though not coherently, like sides one and two of a cassette bleeding together.

* * *

At one point Bittova plays a kalimba, a small wooden box whose metal tines produce dreamy tones. A child calls out from the back of the room. Bittova looks up and answers, "Hello." She scans the crowd hoping to continue the exchange. A few minutes later the boy and his mom are sitting next to me at the counter. A woman on my left smiles and leans back to give the boy a better view. Then his parents change shifts. The boy takes to his dad's shoulder, still beaming.

I envy people who take such cultural risks (*Wow, you brave, adventurous souls, bringing a four-year-old to a show like this!*) as much I judge them (*Come on, you naïve, negligent fools, bringing a four-year-old to a show like this?*). Where do Allie and I fall on the continuum of exposing and protecting?

* * *

George Carlin: "Have you ever noticed when you're driving that anyone who's driving slower than you is an idiot, and anyone driving faster than you is a *maniac*? See, look at this idiot here, will you just look at this idiot just creeping along! Whoa, look at that maniac go!"

* * *

Bittova continues to roam the room, encouraging people to respond, join in, participate. She seeks out the boy and taps him on the shoulder but recognizes that he's grown too tired to engage. The kid may be drowsy but he's at ease with the show, as are so many others. The couple to my right is passing sticky notes back and forth, pointing, grinning, laughing. When I try to track down photos after the show, Holly Bogdanffy writes that she and Michael were too enthralled to take many pictures. I'm still trying to shape it, mold it, solidify an experience perhaps best left in gaseous form. There's a gap between my thoughts and reactions.

* * *

Last week a colleague at school showed me a new way to multiply numbers. Instead of digits she drew intersecting lines to represent numbers. It was like nothing I'd seen before, like random scratches that formed a city map-like grid. It took a few attempts before anything came into focus and even then I wasn't sure what to do. Share it with students? Polish it for a parlor trick? I was trying to decide what to do with this new strategy but it had already made its mark—reset my boundaries, reminded me yet again that there will always be different tactics, different ways to nudge the fence lines ever outward.

* * *

I came across this jot in my notebook. I think it's from an episode of Marc Maron's *WTF* podcast. "Theory of phenomenology—people need to encounter things that reawaken the senses."

* * *

Bittova encores with "My Funny Valentine." She initiates a call and response. Like any good improv it's rooted in "Yes, and"—agree to the premise and add information. She goes back and forth with someone sitting up front three or four times until the responder can no longer up the ante, can't muster another "and" and just belts out, "Bah!"

The room is still crowded when I run into Eric. "The shows just keep getting better," he says, "What'd you think?" I don't have a ready response. I'm still thinking about the performance, searching for the right words, wishing that I shared more of his certainty and excitement.

Daniel Levin | Michael Bogdanffy-Kriegh

Aquanauts Fading from View
Daniel Levin & Juan Pablo Carletti

"Every sha la la la
Every whoa oh oh oh
Still shines"
—The Carpenters, "Yesterday Once More"

Some improvisers warm up, take a reading or two at the start of a set, check their bearings. Others hurtle to fathomless depths, react and respond as they plummet, pulling all bystanders, innocent or otherwise, in with them. Daniel Levin (cello) and Juan Pablo Carletti (percussion) have chosen the latter.

Levin thumps his fist on the body of his cello, then saws away, excavates profoundly satisfying, reedy sounds. How does the wood withstand such pummeling and not splinter? Carletti's mallets roll like thunder back and forth between his floor and rack toms. I need a chance to breathe but Levin and Carletti will have nothing of it. The sunlight zone is fading from view and with it many of the things we use to acclimate ourselves. We're sealed in for a delightfully disorienting ride.

* * *

Comic book artists use the term "gutters" when referencing the white space between panels. I never noticed them before reading Douglas Wolk's *Reading Comics*. He details how gutters give greater definition to the panels that precede as well those that follow. They also call on the reader to do some of the lifting. "The gutter is where the fun happens… readers get to fill in the lapse in time."

* * *

Every time I look at Carletti he has something different atop his snare drum—bells, chimes, cymbals. He even leans back and puts his foot up there to mute the drum before dropping out of sight to pick up something that I mistake for a harmonica. When he pops up, still on high alert, he's back to the brushes. Meanwhile, Levin bear hugs his cello, and shakes his head wildly pursuing dark, rich sounds. He and Carletti push each other downward, a two-person submersible that descends past the point where sunlight reaches, down near the hydrothermal vents where water gushes out at 850 degrees yet doesn't boil due to the soul crushing pressure.

* * *

Maine, part one: One of my first record buying experiences was in Bangor, visiting my fraternal grandparents. We went to Freese's department store, and I found a bin of $3.99 albums. I bought two. The Genesis record, *…and Then There Were Three*, was clogged with gobs of syrupy keyboards; I couldn't find the songs. The E.L.O. record, an early best-of, contained some of Roy Wood's madman cello antics; I couldn't escape the songs—those woofer-punishing frequencies glued themselves to my psyche.

* * *

The duo pulls back. Levin delicately plucks. Carletti rotates his sticks, holds them vertically, and stirs the perimeter of his floor tom, then trades for a mallet to gently tap the top hi-hat cymbal. The eye of the hurricane, a gutter.

* * *

Maine, part two: My friend Mike lives in Orono. He had friends visiting from New York and they stopped at a gas station convenience store (ironically called The Big Apple). The friend, accustomed to city-sized delis and bodegas, was blown away by the amount of unused space in the store, the vast acres between and at the end of aisles. He said he felt like he'd landed on another planet.

* * *

I used to have an aversion to white space. In music, on the screen or on the page, blank space amounted to wasted opportunities. I sought out music that was full throttle, full time. When friends and I made zines we crammed every square inch with material—clip art, lists, captions, random minutiae. I loved zines like Rev. Nørb's *Sick Teen*, hand-stapled pages buzzing with squint-till-it-aches four-point fonts and impenetrable layers of clip art, marathon sentences and parenthetical clauses that were like a new form of surrealism. I disliked, maybe even resented, the abundance of empty space often employed in fancier, bound magazines like *Punk Planet*. I thought it was egregious, almost boastful—*We've got space and, by extension, money to burn.* I didn't see the thought and expression in such an aesthetic, nor did I recognize my opportunity to slow down and absorb.

* * *

Carletti removes the top hi-hat cymbal, strikes it, and lets it resonate before setting the cymbal on the floor tom. Levin reaches down and pinches a string near the bridge. A moment later he lifts his cello to his lap and pushes his bow across the leg that supports the cello. Now he's holding two bows, playing above and beneath the strings. The duo's first set is comprised of three pieces. The second, so far, just one. Fewer gutters. Quicker clip. More time down below.

* * *

Jacques Cousteau once tried, in the '60s, to develop an underwater colony. The first of these continental shelf stations, Conshelf I, was set off the coast of France. The goal was to allow small crews—aquanauts—to live and work there for weeks at a time.

* * *

The way Levin and Carletti exchange ideas so fluidly is like two parts of the same instrument. Talking with Levin he says, "It's like I think [Juan Pablo] is playing cello." Or at least that's what I hear. Later I follow up with Levin. "I don't remember exactly what I said, but it is more to do with navigating our improvisation using a common language of rhythmic ideas and gestures rather than cello vs. drums like a traditional tenor sax vs. drums scenario. Much more like I use the cello percussively. Juan Pablo provides a backdrop and I paint over it in large brush strokes."

Their collaboration feels like a long, wide comic strip panel being drawn as the paper comes off the roll. Or maybe a Wes Anderson movie where the camera leads a character across the scene, allows us to walk alongside them. Or perhaps the inverse, a Spike Lee dolly shot, the character stationary and the camera back pedaling toward us, allowing us to see their world as it passes by.

* * *

Costeau's underwater experiments were largely successful. The researchers were active and content as they conducted experiments within and beyond their underwater dwelling. But they learned that they were unable to remain submerged indefinitely because they couldn't live without sunlight.

* * *

Tonight Levin and Carletti have fashioned the latest version of Conshelf: Quinn's. And even now, as the show comes to end and we hang out and run post-game analysis, it seems sustainable. I see Eric and finally pass along the book I've been keeping in my car. Steve updates me on the house renovations he and his wife have been doing and introduces me to Dan, who knows the same pool of Central and Western New York punk bands that I came up with in the '90s. We're collectively content in the cozy confines of Conshelf: Quinn's.

Then this:

> "Every shing-a-ling-a-ling
> That they're starting to sing's so fine"

Damn it. Someone's playing the Carpenters. Loudly. We've sprung a leak. The bubble's going to burst, and there's no choice but to resurface.

Eric Porter, patron

I was never a bar person. I enjoyed going to the city, going to museums, going to classical and opera, going to the theatre. I never was a club guy. The change of lifestyle changed that. When I moved here to Beacon, just coming out of a divorce, the single life and living right next to a bar. I'm a smoker, so I would come outside of Dogwood and have my cigarettes and talk with people outside. [laughs] It was probably six months before I actually went inside the bar.

As I became acquainted and started meeting more friends, a lot of local musicians, I would come to Quinn's on the other nights—outside of the jazz night—to be supportive of the other local musicians, although the music I didn't enjoy.

Alan "Juice" Glover, I have known him for years and he was a big influence for me wanting to hear more live jazz. When I told him William Parker was going to be here he told me that he was William's mentor at The Firehouse. I invited Juice and his wife. They had a great night. I'm inviting friends all the time. I try to be here every Monday and just been amazed at the talent.

* * *

I grew up in a civil rights household. My father was a Baptist minister and president of the NAACP. Our church was the center of the civil rights movement. I grew up in Meridian, Miss., which is near where the three civil rights workers were killed in Philadelphia [Miss.] in 1964. James Chaney, the black civil rights worker, was my neighbor. The Freedom Summer of 1964, where many white college students were trained to come down to the rural south to do education, but more so they would go into the rural communities to encourage blacks to vote. James Chaney was involved and Mickey Schwerner was training some of the local people to help with registration drives.

James Chaney and Mickey Schwerner had dinner in our home the night before they left for Philadelphia. I was seven years old at the time, and just as I'm talking here to you, I remember them saying their pleasantries, goodnight, after dinner. And years later my father told me that he tried to convince them not to go to Philadelphia because he knew that their lives were in danger because the KKK had a contract out on Mickey Schwerner. I said to my father aren't you glad you didn't convince them not to go because they became martyrs. That event is probably one of the ten most important events in American history. That changed America. That moved us towards that more perfect nation that our founding fathers intended. Even though our founding fathers were just as racist. [laughs] That event changed America because it woke up white Americans to the plights of blacks in the South.

* * *

Our family was the first to integrate some of the schools, even before they forced integration. My brothers and sisters went to white schools when we were the only blacks; being called niggers and nobody even wanted to sit next to us, or have lunch with us, or stand next to us.

I started grade school at the black school. Segregated school. The way they implemented the 1954 *Brown versus Board of Education* is that parents could sign up to send their kids to the black school or the white school. I was seventh of twelve kids, and my parents signed me up for fifth grade at a white elementary school that I passed by every day going to the black elementary school. The white elementary school was right at the top of the hill.

Many evenings we would meet at the church and the elderly women, who probably had less than a third grade education, would ask us to tell our stories of how we were treated that day. At the schools. I remember these old ladies being such an encouragement. Telling us that we were somebody. Telling us you don't have to talk back, you don't have to say anything even when they call you nigger. Even if they say ugly things to you, or they spit on you. Don't fight back. It was amazing. My parents knew the importance of education. Even if things were not always fair, they knew that would at least give us a chance.

It wasn't until 1970 that they actually forced integration and integrated the schools throughout Mississippi. It did get better. Even though, it's funny, the whites and the blacks at my school still cannot come together to have their class reunion. I graduated in 1975 and they have separate reunions for blacks and whites. I am going to the white class reunion this weekend. [laughs]

I stayed at an Airbnb in July when I was attending the black fortieth class reunion. Come to find out the lady who owned the place went to high school with me. A white classmate, that's who I stayed with! I told her to get the information for the white reunion to me, to have them invite me. I invited myself, and I said what you ought to do is try to invite more of the blacks. Any of the blacks you may know, invite them.

It's funny I can only remember four [white] friends that I really had a friendship with, a relationship. Jimmy Holford, George Reedy, George

Neville, and Brad Keevin. I'm sure I had other relationships but I've stayed in contact with the four of them. Jimmy is probably the best story that I have. As a young kid, fifth grade, when Martin Luther King was shot, I walk into the classroom the next day and Jimmy does this: he puts a gun to his neck [makes gunshot noise], all excited that Martin Luther King has been shot. But just an amazing guy, I have much respect for him. Because it made me realize that all of these kids—they were taught to be racist. They learned hatred. From their parents. One of the reasons I love sports so much is because even when I went to that school in the fifth grade at recess we'd play kickball, and all that hatred went right away.

* * *

I have to admit that I probably had a hatred for white women growing up. I love to read history books, especially about blacks and our struggle. I read the autobiography of Charles Evers, who was a civil rights leader in Mississippi, and he shared the story about seeing his friend get lynched because a white woman screamed rape after she got caught having sex with a black guy. And I just had this…dislike for white women. I've evolved. I used to have a big prejudice. I didn't like to see mixed, interracial couples. For years. Even when I was married, I'd be in restaurants and if I saw an interracial couple, I would fume. My ex-wife would have to calm me down. She had evolved a lot further than I.

It was almost visceral. "What in the world are they doing together?" Being an engineer and usually being the only black person at the table, in the room, being around white folks a lot more in my professional career, I probably shed a lot of my prejudices. I shed a lot of my prejudice for interracial couples when I had daughters and I was living in predominantly white neighborhoods. I was trying to prepare myself if my daughter came home with a white boyfriend, what would I do? They haven't dated any white men, although I don't think I would have a problem with it. I've evolved.

And then being here, in this area, I've evolved a lot more because even in the Beacon area—although there are quite a few blacks in this area—they don't leverage a lot of this transition that is happening in the Beacon area. The blacks aren't leveraging or benefitting from a lot of the art stuff. You just don't see many blacks out here. I haven't been able to try to figure that out.

I have been writing a book called *The Gospel According to Eric* for about fifteen years. I have about three or four hundred pages. I don't know if I want to publish. I may leave it to my children. I don't consider myself to be a scholar. But I've read the Bible in its entirety probably three or four times. I certainly have an opinion on theology. Most of my writing is related to theology. I'm extremely liberal, probably almost considered a heretic. I am not agnostic nor am I atheist; I would probably still be considered kind of a Christian, although I don't like to be called Christian.

First of all, the Bible is not the inherent word of God as most fundamental Christians believe. I don't believe that. I don't believe in this virgin birth, of the resurrection, which is fundamental to the born-again Christians. These are the tenets of the faith that I grew up with.

I wish my father was still alive. He was an intellectual. Philosopher, great thinker, progressive. He wasn't your typical southern Baptist preacher preaching fire-and-brimstone. I imagine he probably would have had some kind of transformation. Because this idea that Jesus is the only way to this so-called salvation—I have somewhat abandoned that. So that was probably why the divorce occurred. Besides the infidelity, the kind of fundamental Christian foundations fell apart and my wife is extremely conservative in her theology. Firm believer that the Bible is the word of God. She saw me changing, and I think she just felt like her foundation was being crumbled underneath her. She was aware of it, more than I was. She was so spot on about it. Incredible woman. I will love her the rest of my life.

Ravish Momin | Michael Bogdanffy-Kriegh

Around the World in Eighty Minutes
Tarana

"So laid back but so uptight"
—Sebadoh, "The Freed Pig"

"Everything is all right / Uptight"
—Stevie Wonder, "Uptight"

The leaves are changing. Greens to reds, oranges, and yellows. There's a chill in the air and it's getting dark early. For the first time in months I have to turn on the headlights as I drive to Beacon. It's starting to feel like autumn but I'm not ready.

* * *

Lately I've been waking up with the sense that I'm further behind—at work, at home—than I was the day before, and I'm not sure I'm ready for Tarana either. They're an unlikely duo—a drummer and trombonist who incorporate laptops, samplers, synthesizers, and live loops. On its face the lineup is a longshot, the details too disparate to conjoin. Ravish

Momin, Tarana's drummer and spokesman, uses the phrase "folk music from nowhere." This could easily and accurately be revised to "folk music from everywhere."

One of my first notes says, "New Delhi + New Orleans + 'Autobahn.'" My inner cynic squirms. Is this going to derail into "everything *and* the kitchen sink," a multi-genre hodgepodge desperate to display diverse tastes? But those reservations are more radar blip than looming threat. It's impressive how well and how often Tarana reign in those diverse elements.

* * *

Richard Brautigan's *The Hawkline Monster* follows the unlikely duo of Greer and Cameron, a pair of mercenaries traveling from Hawaii to eastern Oregon in 1902. They're hired guns. Greer prefers a 30:40 Krag and he jokes with Cameron about his choice of weapons, a 25:35 Winchester. Greer and Cameron are men of few words. As killers they're also unlikely protagonists. But they're bound by compatible temperaments and shared goals; who they are as individuals is eclipsed by what they do and how.

* * *

Tarana, like any worthy partnership, have an unspoken dynamic of their own. Part of this is rooted in their stage personas. Momin is extroverted, talkative on stage and off. Five minutes into a conversation you'll know his background. (He's lived in India, Hong Kong, London, and the Middle East.) You'll know his outlook on music. ("You know four on the floor, right? Why not seven or thirteen?").

* * *

Game three of the Royals/Orioles series was rained out. I was hoping to follow the game, check the score between songs.

* * *

Rick Parker may speak less on stage, but he's no less a presence. His trombone booms across the room, a big, breezy tone with wave after wave of echoes following in its wake. Then he trades the cool currents of brass for bone-rattling synthesizer blasts, hunching over a keyboard no bigger than a power strip. When he reverts to the trombone he points the slide downward, toward the pedals at his feet, taming them, keeping them in check, maintaining a clear "organic > inorganic" hierarchy.

* * *

"Greer and Cameron had an aura about them that they could handle any situation that came up with a minimum amount of effort and resulting in a maximum amount of effect." —*The Hawkline Monster*

* * *

Momin and Parker run the ROY G BIV gamut, color outside the lines with a wide spectrum of sounds and a fluid economy of motion. Their work-to-outcome proportions rival Greer and Cameron's, less the body count. Yet for all of the samples and echoes and pyrotechnics, it's the drums and trombone, the fundamentals, that keep bringing me back.

* * *

The Royals are in the playoffs for the first time in nearly thirty years. I watched their bandwagon from afar as they squeaked into the playoffs. I jumped on board during the late innings of their comeback against the A's. Then they knocked off the Angels, the best team in baseball, brushed them aside in three straight, each game better than the last. There's a growing sense that they might make it to, even win, the World Series. But more important than the destination is each improbable stop along the way.

* * *

Momin sings a line and loops it. The line repeats as he kicks quarter notes on the bass drum. Parker resumes playing trombone and Momin shifts to a syncopated snare/kick pattern. Just as the ground starts to feel firm Parker trades trombone for synth, segues into sounds bubbly and expansive. I've nearly caught up, nearly finished surveying the scenery, when these sublime bass reports break through. Momin changes tempos, accelerates to fills that roll across the toms. He too operates a battery of electronics, which he triggers with foot pedals. Back and forth they go, filling the room with kaleidoscopic sounds.

* * *

Outfielders Lorenzo Cain and Nori Aoki have become my favorite Royals. Together they patrol thousands of square feet. Cain plays centerfield. In the past week I've seen him make at least three highlight reel catches. He can formulate and act on a plan so swiftly, as if he's calculated his destination before taking his first stride.

Aoki plays right field. In the past week I've seen him nearly turn at least four routine plays into miscues. He charges line drives too fast, nearly overruns them. He takes the most meandering routes to fly balls. What, if anything, is he thinking? He has an uncanny ability to turn the ordinary into the nailbiting.

* * *

Momin and Parker cover even more ground than Cain and Aoki. They leapfrog across continents and timelines mixing traditional and progressive American forms with dub and Indian influences and electronics—East and West, looking back and looking ahead. Tarana keep conjuring different places, different regions, effortlessly trotting around the globe. My mental map is covered with push pins and a network of criss-crossing yarn.

* * *

Cain is African-American. Aoki is Japanese. All too often African-American athletes are described as "natural" and "graceful," as if they merely coast on intuition. The implications being, among other things, that they lack intelligence and/or work habits; their talents are innate rather than cultivated. The stereotypes of Asian athletes lie at the other end of the continuum; through intellect and diligence they maximize what they were born with. Cain and Aoki undermine those stereotypes, muddy the waters, which only enhances their appeal.

* * *

Director Lizzie Borden, interviewed on The Projection Booth podcast, said she intended her films to portray alternate takes on feminism. Her characters lived on the fringes of society and she wanted to show that their compasses, though of different design, aligned with those of their mainstream counterparts. She didn't want to shoehorn words or attitudes into their experiences for the sake of gaining a wider audience. "Why should we put words in the mouths of women who believe the same things? Why should they speak our language? We should have simultaneous languages."

* * *

Ravish Momin says he's been accused of selling out with Tarana, playing it too straight with the use of steady beats, though it's hard to overlook the many unexpected choices Tarana pile atop those rhythms. It's also difficult to imagine someone using a drums/ trombone/electronics band to pave the way to fame and fortune. Tarana are fluent in many simultaneous languages—musical and cultural—and arguably forging their own.

There's a problem with my credit card when I settle up at the end of the night and I'm out of cash. "Don't worry about it." Mark says. "Get it next time." My sense of relief carries over as I leave, noticing the vines on the bank across the street. Despite the hour the leaves are unusually green, vibrant. From parts unknown I hear crickets, and it feels warmer than it has all day.

Sarah Bernstein | Michael Bogdanffy-Kriegh

Not Quite Fully Past and Gone
Iron Dog

"Ain't it funny how we waste our days?"
—Badlands, "Waste"

There's nothing quite like a quiet day at home, especially a sunny sweatshirt autumn day. It's also Rosh Hashanah, so there's no school. I'm catching up on house projects when Richard arrives, his truck filled with firewood. The image of his battered pick-up with the handmade sidewalls dumping firewood on the driveway should evoke cozy winter fires, blankets, cocoa, and soft falling snow. Instead I see a massive, splintery pile of disorder and an afternoon of stacking wood.

* * *

Iron Dog take the stage and take the place by storm, albeit a storm that forms slowly before opening up. They're from Brooklyn. Sarah Bernstein (violin, vocals), Stuart Popejoy (bass), and Andrew Drury (drums). Initially it's like a three-ring circus, each band member in their own spotlight, my attention alternating from one to the next.

My first notes make little sense. One reads:

> Violin = 16 rpm
> Drums = 33 1/3 rpm
> Bass = 45 rpm

Another says:

> Drums = nomads of ancient Northern Africa
> Bass = ships of Zhu De
> Violin = strings of Renaissance Europe

* * *

Slowly, piece after piece, the wood clunks into the wheelbarrow. The driveway pile shrinks as the garage stacks rise. I square the ends and fill the middle, wood chips snagging on my work gloves. I have music on but it's not loud enough to mask the sounds of leaves crunching underfoot and rustling overhead. I'm surprised by how satisfying the work is. (Don't white collar types always say such things when their manual labor is optional and occasional?)

* * *

Stuart Popejoy stands in the glow of a red neon sign. His legs are locked in place and he bends every which way at the waist, Reed Richards freed from the lab. Popejoy holds his bass nearly upright and both hands are in constant motion, so fast and fluid. His sound is malleable—clean, then distorted, then synth-like—and always there to connect the other elements. He stares at the ceiling, looks up and beyond. I'm ready for his eyes to roll back into his head and for him to speak in tongues.

Technically, Andrew Drury is the drummer but he's revised the job description, just as much a player of strings and brass as percussion. He bows a dust pan, then a piece of sheet metal. He pushes the bottoms of his sticks across the head of the floor tom. He turns a faucet fixture into a mouthpiece, places it on the head of the same drum, and blows. Later he performs mouth-to-drum resuscitation, rotating his floor tom ninety degrees, holding it in his lap, and using the tiny hole on the side as a mouthpiece, rendering the thing a woodwind. But the *Sanford and Son* equipment is only a means to an end, the output more interesting than the tools.

Sarah Bernstein plays strings (violin) and sings, part John Cale, part Nico. Standing behind a semi-circle of effects pedals, her sound ranges as far as those of her bandmates. She leaps about the upper layers, skips across the canopy of the band's sound. When she interjects lyrics, they're more spoken than sung. I can't make much literal sense of the words. They volley between serious comments and "for the sake of the sound" non-sequiturs, something else to ponder when sorting through the sonics. Here's one I like: "improper contest attire."

* * *

When I was growing up our neighbors had a circular, above ground pool. When we walked or swam in the same direction we could create a mini-whirlpool; the water swirled round and round and the current carried us along.

* * *

For all of the band's individual prowess, Iron Dog are best when they all push in unison, generate a different kind of whirlpool. How they decide when and how to converge is mysterious. One moment they're circling around one another. The next there they are, a three-person flash mob converging in the corner of a restaurant.

* * *

So many things feel like they're winding down, closing up for the season. The patio furniture is stacked and stored. Temperatures are dropping, the Mets are playing out their final games, and my Mom moved out last weekend. The house-to-apartment transition flies by, months of phone calls and emails, debates and discussions dissolve in a few hours.

As the truck is unpacked—boxes, then furniture—Mom directs traffic from the kitchen table. We shuffle and reposition and restack, try to control the boxes flowing in through the front door—a 3-D Tetris. We are also prepared to smooth the way emotionally, put her at ease, and try once more to sell the virtues of the new apartment. But there isn't a need. She's moving in and moving on. Within days she's calling to say that she wants to sell the house and soon, that it's time to stop dragging things out. After all that's been dumped on her in recent years she was re-establishing some control.

* * *

The biblical name for Rosh Hashanah is Yom Teruah, which translates to "day of shouting" or "making a noise" or "day of awakening blasts." Iron Dog deal in all three, though forced to pick one, I'd opt for choice C. Some bands stretch boundaries. Others deny the existence of boundaries. Iron Dog use them to gain traction. Rise and shine and thrash the norms.

* * *

From Woody Allen's *Take the Money and Run:*

Bank clerk (Uncredited): "What does this say?"

Fielding Melish (Woody Allen): "Umm, can't you read that?"

Bank clerk: "I can't read this. What's this? *Apt* natural?"

Fielding Melish: "No, it says, *Please put $50,000 into this bag and* act *natural.*"

Bank clerk: (Confirming) "It does say *act* natural."

Fielding Melish: "Uh, I am pointing, uh, a gun at you."

Bank clerk: "That looks like *gub*. That doesn't look like *gun*."

Fielding Melish: "No, it's *gun.*"

Bank clerk: "No, that's *gub*. That's a b."

Fielding Melish: "No, see, that's an *n*. G-u-n. It's *gun.*"

* * *

Here's another of Bernstein's lyrics: "We make lists because we don't want to die."

James catches the line, too. He leans over when he sees me write it down, but he hears it differently: "We *like* lists because we don't want to die."

Between sets we go back and forth, our take on the old Miller Light ad ("Make!"; "No, like!"). We ask Bernstein to settle the debate. She indulges us. She laughs, too, because she can't remember the line from memory and reaches for her lyric sheet. (It's "like," not "make.") They're variations on the same theme, deciphering lyrics and liking lists, different ways to make room and carve out order, overcome the chaos of the day.

Andrew Drury | Michael Bogdanffy-Kriegh

Andrew Drury, musician

I wasn't especially interested in extended techniques until I had a gig in Vancouver with Peggy Lee (the cellist, not the singer), saxophonist Wally Shoup, and a second drummer (just what every quartet needs, right?), Peggy's husband, Dylan Van Der Schyff. It was typical Pacific Northwest weather for February—drab and grey—as saxophonist Wally Shoup and I drove north from Seattle. This was in 2002 or '03.

I confess I had been looking forward to the conversation with Wally on the drives to and from Vancouver as much as the gig itself. For three hours we talked about music and capitalism, Marx, anarchism, oddball artists sprinkled around the U.S. in the '60s and '70s, the Seattle Supersonics basketball team with Payton and Kemp, the Seattle free improvisation scene, Captain Beefheart, Tina Turner, James Carse's book *Finite and Infinite Games*, gigs we'd played in the past, and our more recent doings. It's always great to talk with Wally and witness his deceptively soft Carolina drawl as it skewers and savors meaty chunks of American culture. I guess I was in a searching mood, ready for some new ideas, or new ways of thinking through old ones.

We parked. The neighborhood was green, cold, dripping with moss. Cedar and spruce trees, even the houses themselves, sagged under the weight of rain. Walking into Peggy's house we encountered kids running around, an exquisite graphic music score by Barry Guy framed on the wall, and Dylan expertly managing a large cast iron skillet on the stove gently bubbling with fish curry. Over basmati rice, the spicy orange curry filled us with warmth.

After dinner we headed out via Vancouver's elevated monorail train to the venue—a loft in a seedy district of porno shops and liquor stores—but when we got there Peggy couldn't find her pickup. There wasn't enough time to go back home and get it so she would have to play unamplified. This, to me, meant disaster: over the years I had played with several cellists and it never worked without amplification. Drum set always buries cello and this makes for some boring-to-listen-to music.

I had also had time to reflect on the fact that the cello sounded like a completely different instrument when it was unamplified—far richer, a sound that projects three dimensionally, especially in that opulent, woody low register. A pickup—usually run through a guitar amp—was a procrustean proposition. It didn't convey the sound that makes a cello a cello. It was too bad, tragic, that they had to amplify at all.

And then I had this kind of obvious moral realization: if cellists routinely compromised a major component of their music—their very sound—to play with me then wasn't it reasonable and fair for me in this case to put some limits on my sound to play with a cellist? How many times had I seen a cellist on stage sitting amid electric guitars, drums, and horns, sawing away inaudibly, reduced to being a visual prop? It seemed like this was what people thought a cello was for. Why should cellists always be the ones making the sacrifice?

I thought to myself *"a really GOOD drummer in this situation would be able to make MUSIC."* I imagined Jack DeJohnette or Terry Clark or

Pheeroan Aklaff or some super creative, resourceful, intelligent, virtuosic drummer—not myself by any stretch but some idealized Other—knowing exactly what to do and doing it. A kind of sage of the instrument whose fundamental musicality was so intact it wouldn't matter what s/he was doing on the surface, the result would sound as if it couldn't possibly be any other way. I thought I might as well try to copy what that drummer would do.

I had come a long way—from New York City to Seattle and then north to Vancouver—to play with Peggy so I might as well try something new. I decided to focus on quiet sounds, all the little supposedly non-musical sounds I had noticed over the years, accidental sounds that drum sets make, like when you sit down and something creaks, or after pressing into the drum head you quickly remove your palm from the head and the drum resounds. Rubs, rattles, sounds of adjustments, slow pressure, weight shifting. I think I might have used sheets of crumpled paper as drum sticks that night. And most of all I used silence.

It was a leap into the abyss. My approach was far from perfect that night but the music as a whole, I thought, was really great. It wouldn't have been had I adhered to my lifelong devotion to bebop/free jazz convention. But beyond what I felt to be the success of this particular set I came away from the stage absolutely convinced that I had glimpsed something that would be valid and worthwhile to pursue. I could tell I was barely scratching the surface of something.

Avram Fefer | Michael Bogdanffy-Kriegh

The Things We Do to Find the People Who Think Like Us
Avram Fefer

"That's what's most important if you want to be free:
respect for and exasperation with boundaries."
—Haruki Murakami, *Colorless Tsukuru Tazaki and His Years of Pilgrimage*

Saxophonist Avram Fefer opens with a short phrase and passes it to the rhythm section. The Michaels—Bisio and Wimberly—grab it and go, rebound turned fastbreak. Then they pull back, set up the next play, a trio in top gear from the start. Later Fefer says he told the band to "skip the first set and get to the second and third."

My neighbor, Keith, was able to make it tonight and couldn't have picked a better introduction to Quinn's. Early on, it's evident that this will be a memorable night. Joe McPhee and Iva Bittova sense it. They're among the past performers who have returned tonight as fans. Fefer senses it, too. He takes a moment to snap a photo while bassist Michael Bisio solos. Then Fefer reaches to the ceiling, twists side to side, limbers up, and preps for what lies ahead.

* * *

"You say something true, but high-minded—preferably a couple of things true, but high-minded, to set up the rhythm. Then you deflate the whole lofty mess by saying something really true…that leaves the reader with not just a laugh, but insight." —Art Spiegelman's introduction to Harvey Kurtzman's *Jungle Book*

* * *

Fefer floats on long, sustained thoughts as Bisio eases into a mesmerizing bass line, locks in with Wimberly. They stay within the boundaries but it's not to last, not in this form. They toss aside what's accumulated, let loose a blizzard of ideas, beautiful and messy, too many to track yet too tantalizing to ignore.

The group changes course once more, mixes the melodic and the manic. The rhythm section clicks into a groove, repeats a phrase that I can latch onto, while Fefer takes off, pushes to the upper register, strains just short of piercing. Only as he descends do my shoulders drop and I realize the extent to which my body tensed up during the ascent.

* * *

Curses, a comic by Kevin Huizenga, revolves around the existential adventures of Glenn Ganges. In one story Glenn finds himself golfing with a group of seminary professors. An older professor talks about a recent visit to a bookstore. He looks around at "all the books on display—and (thinks), Behold, the vanity of man!"

To which a younger professor responds, "But in all those books God displays his wonders, too—through human imagination, art, history, ideas…" In theory and in practice I agree with the younger professor. But when I first read *Curses* I sided with the older professor. There is so much produced each year, to read, to watch, to listen to. Why add to the heap? I like to think that I am contributing to a larger conversation but I am merely distracting myself, chasing a red dot across the floor?

* * *

Keith and I arrive early and take a booth about halfway back. It's his first time at Quinn's and he's taken with the place by the time we sit down— the atmosphere, the menu, the prospect of great music on a Monday night. We drove up together but I haven't asked how long he wants to stay. I don't want to ask. He might have to—or want to—leave early. A set departure time will only get stuck in my head, distract me, and I'll spend too much time thinking about what I might miss.

* * *

Fefer and Bisio rest on the side, signaling a Michael Wimberly solo. I see an opening up front and ask Keith if he wants to change seats. His nod says, I'm good right here. By the time I walk up Wimberly has switched to mallets, the white felt streaking the air. Then faster, the mallets like helicopter blades. I stay up front to linger with the sights I'd been missing in back—the various shades of gold on Fefer's well-worn horns, the hairs on Bisio's fraying bass bow, Wimberly's fingertips pushing across his floor tom.

* * *

"In times like these we have to try to stay connected to people. And we have to try to make our own days." —Ben Lerner, *10:04*

* * *

Fefer, Bisio, and Wimberly build bridges early and often. This is evident in how they balance composition and improvisation, artfully deliver and embellish upon Fefer's pop art melodies. It's apparent when Fefer acknowledges his predecessors, covering Rahsaan Roland Kirk's "Volunteered Slavery," talking about traveling with Archie Shepp, and playing with Ornette Coleman. He speaks with such humility and reverence, fosters a sense of inclusion, big tent rather than closed circle. Their bridge building is also evident when Fefer claps on the downbeat, urges us to join, spans what's left of the performer/audience divide. Iva Bittova is up front, calling out on the upbeat, bellowing and beaming. It's a well-timed response and spreads across the room.

* * *

After the show Keith and I settle our tab, ready to head home. We stop by the merch table but no one's there. The band is scattered,catching up with friends and fans. Hundreds of dollars' worth of records and CDs sit unattended. They're available but they're secondary. We find Avram Fefer and go overboard on his records. We do the same with Michael Bisio. If Michael Wimberly had albums for sale we'd have completed the trifecta. Each of them is gracious, genuine. The music's over but it seems like the night's just beginning as the post-show hang gets underway. Keith senses this too and suggests we stay for another drink.

Karl Berger | Michael Bogdanffy-Kriegh

Generous Loops
Karl Berger, Ingrid Sertso, & Ken Filiano

"Sarcasm is the weak at work / Snarky shouldn't even be a word."
—Minus 5, "Sweet"

I have a morning flight out of LaGuardia. It leaves too early to take a train to the airport and a taxi would cost too much. My friend Pedro has been working near LaGuardia for the past several weeks. He routinely leaves long before sunrise. He offers me a ride and before I know it his headlights are gliding up the driveway at half past four. I offer him money for gas, but he declines. I'm extremely grateful and tell him numerous times. He politely changes topics. He'd rather talk about the Mets.

* * *

Vocalist Ingrid Sertso gestures, places her fingers to her lips, like a chef who's found the right blend. Karl Berger's glasses rest on the tip of his nose as he dances behind his vibraphone. He finishes a run, then bounces, skips back to his right just in time to reel off the next one. Sertso tunes into Berger's vibes and runs her fingers across an imaginary keyboard. Between them sits bassist Ken Filiano, harnessing the lighter-than-air sounds of his bandmates.

* * *

I arrive at the airport to find my flight's been delayed, which puts my connecting flight in jeopardy. How am I going to contact the friends who are picking me up in L.A.? I'm tired and hungry and growing impatient. I'm starting to feel the day slip away when I drop my water bottle and accidentally spray the woman standing behind me. I kneel down to clean up and notice that her bag is wet too. Before I can apologize she's handing me a tissue. Then she takes out one for herself and asks if I got any on me.

First Pedro, now the water bottle lady. At every turn the day is marked by uncommon generosity. Even the book I'm reading, Mike Sacks's *Poking a Dead Frog*. Many of the interview subjects are young comedians and comedy writers. It could lapse into a series of chats with the self-satisfied, but his range of subjects and ever-present curiosity are too great. He interviews sitcom pioneer Peg Lynch, ninety-six years old and still writing each day, about *Ethel and Albert*, the radio and TV show she created, wrote, and starred in back in the '40s. Later, when he references old television shows, he provides bits of context ["*Taxi* (1978-1983)"] rather than presume he's preaching to the converted.

* * *

Sertso sits on a stool. A black scarf rests around her neck, a half dozen bracelets on each wrist, her purse hanging from a music stand. She often sings with her eyes closed, like the notes are there to be sensed, felt more than seen. She guides the lyrics, shepherds language into the world. Her lyrics are unflinchingly earnest and the rhythms consistently connect.

"Time is
Time is in
Time is in this
Time is in this if
Time is in this
Time is in
Time
Is
Time is in"

Seeing those lines stretch over and back across the page reminds me of the computer class I took in high school, probably '85 or '86. Dave Finney and I were trying to skate by. We typed up a list of our favorite groups, including his band:

```
10    Kinks
20         Yes
30              Minutemen
40                   Moody Blues
50                        Milk Cow Pumpkin
60                   Traffic
70              Eric Clapton
80         Black Flag
90    Monkees
100   Go to 10
Run
```

We probably did other things in class but I only remember running that basic program, watching the names scroll over and back across the green-on-black screen, then adding more band names. This is the future, we thought dismissively, distracting but useless.

* * *

After each song Sertso, Berger, and Filiano grin at each another. They reach out and clasp hands, call out each other's names. My old punk bands used to exchange looks of pleasant surprise whenever we ended a song in unison. But this trio has been active for decades, landed thousands of songs, and yet each one still merits celebration. They are so generous and supportive. Tonight it's not about bending time signatures or displays of virtuosity. It's not about venturing into the unexpected. It's about reframing the expected.

* * *

During my layover in Dallas I find a charging station for my phone. Still no word from my friends in L.A. As I'm checking the phone's status, I hear a gentle voice over my shoulder. "Excuse me, am I in your way?" I turn to see an elderly woman's kind face. She too is holding a charger. Hers is attached to a portable respirator. A few minutes later, walking away with her family, wheeling her respirator, she stoops over to pick up a candy wrapper that someone else has carelessly dropped.

* * *

Sertso and Berger, sync up, voice and vibes. They match rhythms but it's the combination of their timbres that floats to the foreground. Meanwhile Filiano thumps along, a sound so sweet and reliable and there, always there, the fulcrum on which everything balances. Their music is light and breezy, yet grounded.

It's like watching my kids fly kites on the beach last summer. The kite string was invisible, as if their hands alone maneuvered the kites. They sprinted across the beach, kicking up puffs of sand, running like mad to keep those flimsy plastic sheets aloft. The whole thing seemed like a dream but it was sweat and exertion that led to that wondrous sense of verticality, the trust and gradual release.

* * *

"The joy is in the existence
To know love is to know"

Taken in isolation, Sertso's lyrics give me pause. When combined with the bass and vibraphones, though, the ensuing songs stimulate rather than numb. In lesser hands they might tumble into the ravine of hippy naiveté. But there's something wiser, time tested that keeps them on terra firma. I see another glimpse of this after the show when a fan asks Sertso to buy a CD. She says the disc costs $15. He has a twenty. He waits for her to make change. They chat a bit, chanteuse and fan, and moments later he's saying "keep the change." "Are you sure?" she asks. He is now, and glad of it. It's not a hustle. Not a mind trick. Just part of the routine for a seasoned performer. Likewise when I compliment Berger and he asks if I'd like to be added to their email list. These practical exchanges don't detract from the band's idealism. To the contrary. Moments like these provide contrast, round them as people.

* * *

I arrive late in Los Angeles. My friends were stuck in traffic so they're late, too, just arriving as I get to the curb. My worrying was for naught. They ask if I'm hungry and minutes later we're in a burrito joint in East L.A. They let me pick up the tab and for the first time today I'm able to return a favor.

Ingrid Laubrock and Tom Rainey | Steve Ventura

Another Candle on the Cake
Ingrid Laubrock & Tom Rainey

"The doctors can't tell you anything that your bones don't know"
—The Mekons, "Traveling Alone"

It's early. Saxophonist Ingrid Laubrock and drummer Tom Rainey are still setting up and yet there's already something in the air. The rain has held off. The birthday celebration brewing in back has spread across at least four booths, and Laubrock and Rainey have upped the ante by asking to play without microphones despite the boisterous crowd. High wires, no nets.

There's also this exchange between the couple seated next to me:

Dude, mid-twenties, taller, patchy beard: "I'm never going to get married. My dad's been married—five, six, seven—seven times. I can't even live in the same city for more than a year."

Lady, also mid-twenties, shorter, cat's eye glasses: [laughs] "You'll probably get married when you're, like, forty-five."

She chooses a distant, unimaginable, unreachable number. A number about which anything can said because it's beyond experience and conception, like the thought of living in another solar system. I've passed that unreachable number and I'm feeling a bit removed from my fellow showgoers at the moment—not older just old.

As the revelry in back rises Steve cringes, anticipating the unamplified music that's about to start and how it will be heard yet alone received. "This is going to be tough," he says. James acknowledges the elephant in the room when he introduces the band. "Be generous with your ears," he says and, alluding to Mike, one of the cooks at Quinn's, who is celebrating his thirtieth birthday, "he's very excited to have these two artists here tonight." Read: *Let's join him, shall we? Listen and keep it down to a dull roar.*

* * *

It was my wife's idea to clear away some of the weeds that border the backyard and woods. She wanted to carve out a patio, a shady place to hang out when the rest of the yard roasts in the late summer heat. Lou was the person for the job.

* * *

Ingrid Laubrock's performance has me pinballing through time and space. Her eyes are closed and her cheeks are fully expanded, so much pressure, like the tires on Hunter S. Thompson's convertible Coupe de Ville, inflated to the point where he could "feel every pebble on the highway." She rocks on the tips of black shoes, throwing in the occasional leg kick. Her laces are bright red and I flash from Thompson's Vegas to Dorothy's slippers and the road to Oz. But this isn't escapist fantasy any more than it's gonzo journalism. Imaginative, yes. "Click your heels" or "Get twisted on ether and tequila" and wait for the magic, no. Laubrock's playing isn't triggered by talismans or elixirs. It's more personal, unvarnished and unguarded, born of grit and determination.

* * *

Returning from the bathroom I walk past the birthday party. Mike waves me over. He used to work for my wife and asks how she's doing. Standing among the younger, unfamiliar faces I feel that my visitor's pass is all too apparent and I think of what they might be seeing: *It's one of the old dudes from up front.* They're not alarmed or unwelcoming, and though the feeling is fleeting I sense the distinction. I'm the old guy. I have been for a while. That's not how I see myself. Not yet, not internally. I don't feel old because of chronology or appearance; there's not much I can do about those. But I wonder if I've gained geezer status by virtue of subtle everyday behaviors that I don't notice and can neither name nor avoid.

* * *

Lou planned to level the ground, lay down slate, and build a retaining wall, about three feet high, around the back and sides. On the first day, digging into the topsoil, moving vertically through time, one layer after another, he found glass bottles, shoe soles, and rusty garden tools. Previous owners buried their trash in the woods. We've grown accustomed to finding bits of garbage back there, usually after a heavy rain. Sharp, rusty, and broken. It's junk by any standard. Yet in Lou's hands everything has a backstory and is ready to be reframed, reconsidered. The glass brown medicine bottle would look nice on the kitchen window sill, he says, and the old pitchfork could be wiped off and mounted on the side of the garage.

* * *

Tom Rainey is so quick around the kit and delicate, gentle in a way that the cymbals scarcely move. He swipes and strikes and he's capable of the most unbelievable reaches and stretches. It's like the aerial fight scenes in *Crouching Tiger, Hidden Dragon.* James taps me on the shoulder. He's air drumming, right arm over left, a rapid 1-2, 1-2, oom pah, oom pah beat. "Hardcore punk, man!" Indeed it is and I'd been missing it, stuck in time, still back on Rainey's lightly falling rhythms of a minute ago.

* * *

Initially I wondered how tonight's mix of audience and mic-free music would turn out. But the experience has been undiminished by the party, perhaps enhanced by it. Cue the couple next to me, providing more reassurance than they realize.

Cat's Eye: "I was talking to my dad and he's like, Yeah, you're right, Bernie Sanders is cool. My dad watches Fox but he believes me."

The Nomad: "That's my goal: to convert my mom."

* * *

After two days Lou had filled the back of his truck with debris and made a run to the dump. Then he started finding car parts. Small, at first— cables, a brake pedal, a door handle. But he couldn't remove the handle because it was still attached to a door, and the door was connected to the body of a car. Lou had found an entire car, bumper to bumper, buried in our backyard.

* * *

"[*A Wrinkle in Time*] is not too difficult for kids. It's too difficult for grown-ups. Too many grown-ups tend to put themselves into little rooms

with windows that don't even open and doors that are locked. And they want to close themselves off from any new ideas. And you're ready and open for new ideas and new things and new places and new excitements."
—Madeline L'Engle, from the introduction to the *A Wrinkle in Time* audio book

* * *

Ingrid Laubrock: "A microphone changes the sound, and on top of that the sound comes out of the speakers rather than from the source, the instrument. Also, in a room that small I prefer not to give any control over dynamics to a sound person. We prefer to balance that ourselves. I often want to do stuff that creeps in quietly underneath and is not supposed to be heard until it is quite loud. Often sound people we don't know don't know that—and can't—and assume the saxophone is always on top like a soloist."

* * *

Lou kept digging. He had no intention of excavating the car but he was curious, and he needed to fill any air pockets beneath the patio-to-be, pack them with dirt so that they wouldn't cave in. The car, a Chevy, late '50s or early '60s, was surprisingly well preserved.

* * *

Madeline L'Engle explains there are two types of time in the *Wrinkle in Time* universe. There is *chronos* ("ordinary, wrist-watch, alarm-clock time") and *kairos* ("real time, pure numbers with no measurement"). Laubrock and Rainey are of the latter, independent of one another, beyond conventional time, never where I expect them to be. They each seem to occupy multiple places in any given moment. And yet they're so unified, always together, soaring and trusting like acrobats, lighter than air but with passages that rattle and shake. Things of this magnitude seldom move with such agility, Vikings in battle gear, vaulting and somersaulting, flying with an unexpected greatest of ease.

Laubrock and Rainey ramp up as they approach the end, bigger, louder, brighter. Then she begins a gradual fade while he sets down his sticks and plays the snare with his fingertips. They have an uncommon ability to lay low, sneak up in plain view, peaking at their most eloquent and stirring.

James takes the mic, glances back at the duo as they pack up. "Maybe we'll see you again here soon. Maybe with two birthday parties? Seemed to work this time."

Mark Pisanelli, former Quinn's bartender, musician

I made the first sale. James Keepnews, Peekskill IPA. I remember saying to Tom [Schmitz], "Here's the first dollar, for the first sale." He's like, "Uh, that's superstition." So I just put it in the register.

* * *

After high school I was playing music regularly and wasn't sure if I should attend college or wait. I remember walking by the Bardovan [Opera House in Poughkeepsie] like, "Wow, I want to work here." I walked in the back, talked to the stage manager and filled out an application. About a month later I was a roadie. I got into doing big shows with top-name acts. Got to meet one of my favorite drummers, Kenny Aronoff, did one for Tony Bennett. At the age of twenty it was a humbling experience. I was confused about what I'd become. Being a drummer with a lot of energy, the only thing I knew was that music was a guiding force. The Bardovan helped me find my place, the stepping stones of being nice.

My friend Alex, we played in our first band together, the Buddha Heroes. We were a good team. I really enjoy learning through music, but I feel like I wasn't ready for college yet and kept working. I felt pressure from my middle class family so I had to rebel. Invented my own ways to do it in kind of a responsible way, through music. I invented my own path through music. I remember watching *Space Ghost: Coast to Coast*. I set up some cardboard boxes and started playing drums to that. That's how I started playing the drums, to *Space Ghost*. With hangers. Cardboard boxes. I was just bashing away. I heard something in the theme song.

* * *

Some jazz nights were hard to get through. No offense, jazz players, but dealing with jazz musicians is really difficult. At first, for someone new to the whole world, they were very demanding.

But the worst, or greatest, thing James ever did to me was expose me to Extreme Thursdays. That stuff was the worst, and he loved it. I would actually get angry. I was like, "I can't do this anymore. This is the worst 'music' I've ever heard. Everyone's leaving." I got to the point where I told the guy who was in one band, "You were horrible." Never in my life had I told a musician that they sucked until then. Steve told them to stop. He told them to freakin' stop. It just struck a chord, an extreme chord.

Extreme Thursdays was the perfect title for that night because it redefined extreme. It made you feel. Just like getting angry while viewing contemporary art. Like Dia art. Are you kidding me? Breaking glass and leaving it in the middle of the floor, you know? As time went on, I surrendered. Quinn's made me a better listener, made me a better player. I realized that even though everyone was different, they all had one thing in common and that was Quinn's. It was a real big therapy session. Karl Berger, he's the vibraphonist? Watching him jump up and down on stage is amazing. I want that spirit.

* * *

My dad took me to Shea Stadium a lot growing up and then eventually Citi Field but even then I never really cared. I never fully understood baseball, or sports in general, because I was so focused on playing music. And then one day I heard that the 2015 Mets won the first eleven games in a row and something clicked. That year was amazing and everyone who worked at Quinn's was a Mets fan. So we were like, "Come on, man, the Mets are in the playoffs! We got to get this TV going." We tried to convince Tom. [laughs] Got cable for a week.

We had those few playoff games and I remember yelling at Steve one night, it was a jazz night. Like, "The game is on! What do you mean we can't watch the game? Are you kidding me?" We compromised. He's like, "Okay, you can only turn it on during the intermission." The staff were pretty much the only ones watching—jazz night crowd, no one really cared. It brought a different group of people to Quinn's for a hot second. With so many bands, stories, drunken nights—and all the frustrations that came with it—I loved Quinn's for what it was. I was grateful to be there.

* * *

I work at Denning's Point Distillery as well as the Soap Company now, two places that weren't here a few years ago. When people come in the distillery they are mainly from the city and I say, "Well, if you want to see what Beacon really looked like in the '90s, just watch *Nobody's Fools* with Paul Newman." You'll see Main Street for what it used to be and you'll see the whole vibe of the city. That held true for my upbringing years. I remember my mom saying, "If you're going to go ride your bike just don't go down Main Street."

My theory is the recession helped Beacon. People moved up from the city and that helped the local economy. At first it was a struggle. "Oh, you're a local?" I hated it at first. I didn't understand the economic gain from all these new faces and not being a dying town anymore. It changed my maturity level. It made me understand the benefits of evolution.

Nostalgic for an Age Yet to Come
Joe McPhee & Graham Lambkin
Plan B from Outer Space

"I'm the last of the soot and scum brigade
And all this peaceful living is driving me insane"
—The Kinks, "Last of the Steam Powered Trains"

The front door closes behind me and I find myself in the sweet embrace of the Kinks' *Village Green Preservation Society* playing over the PA. It's long been one of my favorite records, though its characters yearning for distant days seem antithetical to a night at Quinn's.

"Last of the Steam Powered Trains" fades out and Steve introduces Joe McPhee and Graham Lambkin.

Steve: "You guys ready?"

McPhee: "Ready to launch."

* * *

I experienced a wave of sentimentality as a kid, more so than most I think, especially in eighth grade. My cold war anxieties spiked that year—ABC's *The Day After* didn't help—and my folks split up. I watched *Leave It to Beaver* and *My Three Sons* reruns. I read all that I could find about Jackie Robinson and the Brooklyn Dodgers, and I discovered the Kinks' *Arthur* and *Village Green.* I was nostalgic for an age that had come and gone before I was born. I felt I'd missed out and wanted to be part of a time other than my own.

* * *

Last week there was a message from Joe McPhee on Facebook, previewing tonight's show: "Sound Artist Graham Lambkin and I begin the proceedings with the first set...instrumentation: various 'stuff.'"

McPhee and Lambkin sit across from one another at a table like dinner guests or chess opponents. Between them lies the various stuff, percussion, trumpet, tape recorder, with additional instruments and implements waiting in an open suitcase on the floor. There's also a paper bag. Lambkin holds a maraca in one hand and a microphone in the other. He has a serene look, like my dad, circa '76, pressing soldering iron to circuit board, assembling a television from a kit. Lambkin places the mic on the speaker of a tabletop cassette player. High tide lapping against a dockside boat. Then an enveloping rumble, a subway passing next door. As the sound fades he reaches for the paper bag and slowly, slowly crumples it.

* * *

Joe McPhee plays a bit of trumpet but focuses primarily on synthesizer and percussion, instruments I've never seen him play. Theoretically this change could be construed as a lost opportunity, like Willie Mays hawking hot dogs rather than patrolling centerfield.

Then again I should know by now the extent to which McPhee feeds on the unexpected. After the show someone next to me says that "Joe's still finding his way." McPhee's constant striving is what makes him so compelling. He is uncommonly open to exploration—his energy and drive, the flow of ideas and need for next steps. I've seen him eight times since that first show with Dominic Duval. Each show has been unique, different musicians and instrumentation. And then there are the new releases that continue to stream forth. I relish trying to keep up.

A couple of weeks ago I saw Joe pull James aside. I wasn't trying to eavesdrop but I didn't walk away either. "…Should record before the show…fifty copies…only available at Quinn's…friend in Austin… cassette label…no download…*Science Friction*…" I missed the context—he could have been referring to two or three different projects— but was drawn to the urgency.

McPhee, at the conclusion of the first set: "Thanks for letting us extend our childhoods."

* * *

McPhee, overheard at a recent show at Catalyst Gallery: "Don't give me that 'legend' bullshit. It makes me feel like I have one foot in the grave."

* * *

"He's a sailing captain, zigging and zagging his whole life. He doesn't know how to go straight." —Peter Matthiessen, *Far Tortuga*

* * *

"Last of the Steam Powered Trains" plays again between sets. I've listened to this song since I was a teenager but the lyrics have a different tone tonight, less fatigue and resignation, more rolled up shirt sleeves and resilience.

* * *

"[Nostalgia] came into existence as a side effect of imperialism. The people who were sent to take things from other people started missing the things they'd had at home. Swiss mercenaries were the first people diagnosed with it, for a long time scientists even thought it was unique to the Swiss—one theory was that the folk songs and breakfast foods of Switzerland were so good that it did physical harm to remove someone from them." —Mickey Hess, *The Nostalgia Echo*

The nostalgia of my teen years was more ointment than ailment. Thinking back I see that I pulled out of the nosedive by joining the track team, going to movies with friends, and adding contemporary music to my diet. I found ways to look around rather than behind.

* * *

Part two of McPhee's show preview, from the same post: "Set 2, PLAN B FROM OUTER SPACE: James Keepnews (guitar/bass/laptop), Dave Berger (drums), Joe McPhee: More 'stuff.' Plan B is that there is no plan! We are improvisers and every day of our lives has been a rehearsal for December 8th at Quinn's, 'THE NEW FIVE SPOT ON THE HUDSON.'"

* * *

This is from "Montage," a song from Trey Parker and Matt Stone's *Team America*:

> "Show a lot of things happening at once
> Remind everyone of what's going on
> To show it all would take too long
> If you fade out it seems that more time has passed in a montage..."

* * *

Seeking out still more live music, James and I recently ventured into New York City. We met for barbeque in Manhattan and took the L train to a bookstore in Ridgewood. We browsed used paperbacks, watched a band, headed back to Manhattan for a drink, got in line for a second show, left the line and went to the pizza place next door because we were too early, and hung out in the neighborhood after the show because we were too amped up to go home. Eventually we headed back to Grand Central, saw that we were early for our train, walked to a place on Third Avenue for a drink, talked too long and had to make a mad dash to catch the train in time.

* * *

James bends over the table, now home to his laptop. Mouse in hand, he runs a test, his face illuminated by the laptop, before walking around to check connections. His guitar and laptop offer a galaxy of possibilities, gentle strums yielding thunderclaps, giving way to dream-like swirls of no fixed origin.

Dave Berger counts time on the hi-hat, steady clicks with kick drum punctuation. Whatever restraint Joe McPhee demonstrated earlier evaporates; he torches the place, one nerve-knocking run after another. The trio flies forward, then in reverse, blurring headings, scrambling every dial on the instrument panel, consulting maps and tossing them aside. Yet still a shared course, eyes to the horizon.

* * *

And that is the abbreviated version of our night on the town. James had originally proposed including a movie, too. Usually that's my role. When I meet friends for a show I want to add on a drink or dinner. And if the plan calls for dinner and a show, then I'm checking out movie times.

And if those are in place, then I'm scoping out the nearest bookstore. I relish spending time with people whose thirst for culture and experience matches or exceeds mine.

* * *

James picks up a slide and refracts everything in new directions. Joe and Dave are right there, only to collide and ricochet once more. Joe switches to trumpet, slows the pace, quotes and bends "Old Eyes." Berger focuses on the rack tom and James chimes in with the lightest of adornments. It's profoundly satisfying to see friends, people who've grown closer as a result of Quinn's, on stage creating together.

* * *

"Last of the Steam Powered Trains" is playing yet again as I leave.

"Huff and puff till I blow this world away
And I'm going to keep on rolling till my dying day"

It seems the perfect soundtrack for looking ahead.

All Going Out Together
Jason Kao Hwang's Sing House

"And everybody gets a little piece of the pie"
—The Arrivals, "Simple Pleasures in America"

Andrew Drury picks up a small, metal object, part of a sink faucet he found on a construction job. He leans over his floor tom, places the faucet on the drumhead and exhales. He works with care and precision, a jeweler placing loupe to gem, magnifying what lies within, revealing mournful, voluminous sounds. A solo sans sticks.

Sing House listens and waits. Bandleader Jason Kao Hwang brings his violin to his chin. Trombonist Steve Swell raises his mouthpiece to his lips. Drury continues. Hwang and Swell start nodding to the implied beat, they're ready to come in. And Drury continues. Hwang and Swell rest their instruments. Everyone has a voice in Sing House and right now Drury has more to say. It's a different way to give the drummer some.

* * *

The stage is crowded, more so than usual. I've seen a lot of duos and trios at Quinn's, along with a handful of quartets. This is the first five-piece. More important than the number of names on the scorecard, though, is the scope and range of the personalities, and when everyone is playing, thumping and bumping and wailing and flailing, there is so much to take in, so many places for the eye and ear and mind to go.

Yet for all the activity, the scene takes me back to one of Adrian Chi's *Bite the Cactus* comics, a particularly pensive one called "Drawn to the Desert." The panels depict the before and after of Chi's move from the city of Toronto to the suburbs of Los Angeles, from stimulating to numbing. Then she makes friends and starts taking weekend camping trips, discovers Joshua Tree and Matilija Falls, Death Valley and King's Canyon. "The incredible majesty of these places made the suburbs seem far away and insignificant. There's an indescribable ecstasy sitting in the desert, hiding in the shade of a boulder, that draws me back again and again."

* * *

Steve Swell's eyes are closed, his face clenched. His right hand, bandaged from a recent surgery, looks like a boxer's before the gloves go on. He jabs rapidly, desperately pushing and pulling the slide on his trombone. But there's more to Swell's brand of the sweet science than just the number of punches thrown. Location and impact count too.

I run into Swell a few weeks later. He asks, "Those other things you write about, are you thinking about them while you're listening to the music or do they come to you later?"

I've been writing these essays for months. They've occupied so much of my thinking, but no one's asked so directly about one of their basic components. His question surprises me more than it should. He says the pieces are like schizophrenia.

"I don't mean schizophrenia in all its bad connotations but, I believe this, there can be 'good' schizophrenia. When we play music or write poetry we are dealing with everything we already know or have been exposed to up to that moment just before the actual act of making music or writing poetry. It's all we have to work with. We shut off the learning part and turn on the working part. All the information, disparate as it may seem, comes to the fore when we are creating."

* * *

Chi's comics appear in *Razorcake*, a non-profit punk magazine based in Los Angeles. *Razorcake* captivates me for a number of reasons. Their contributors embrace and repudiate the stereotypes of punk culture. They cover loud, aggressive music filled with no-holds-barred lyrics. They also bring to bear considerable intelligence and a willingness to contemplate. In a recent column *Razorcake* co-founder Sean Carswell used the phrase "Meditate on this with me." Not "react with me" or "get angry with me," but rather "think with me." The zine offers an invitation to explore and reset.

* * *

Bassist Ken Filiano solos. The fingertips of his left hand shift in small increments, balancing on the strings beneath. His right hand goes Nadia Comaneci, leaping above and below his left—low then high, high then low, faster as he goes—plucking harmonics with each perfect landing.

The ensemble resumes, frenetic movement abounds. Just when they might become too divergent, overextended, Filiano repeats a phrase, reshapes and redirects, like Hercules digging a trench to reroute a river.

Between sets Filiano and I talk about books. Larry McMurtry's *Walter Benjamin at the Dairy Queen* comes up. McMurtry writes about being in his sixties, still trying to balance life as a reader with life as a writer;

when he reads a lot he feels that he's neglecting his writing and vice versa. Filiano recommends *Lonesome Dove*. "He doesn't create his characters, he listens to them."

Jason Kao Hwang mirrors this with his Sing House compositions. It's remarkable how well this cast of characters functions together. In that sense Hwang reminds me of Gabriel Byrne's character in *The Usual Suspects*, orchestrating a group of diverse personalities. I'm tempted to match up the five members of Sing House with their counterparts in *The Usual Suspects* but who'd be Stephen Baldwin?

* * *

Christopher Forbes sits at his keyboard, momentarily on the periphery, sizing up the situation, contemplating his options. He pulls his fingertips across the keys, one brush stroke at a time. Then a surge, playing at incalculable, reckless speeds, but always surefooted; nimble within the turmoil, a dazzling combination of velocity and grace. The classic game is set aside for blitz chess.

Visually, Forbes fits the image I have of Lenny Angrush from Jonathan Lethem's *Dissident Gardens*. It's the combination of beard and glasses, upturned pork pie hat and jacket less than pressed. Lenny's a chess hustler and well-read idealist. He's also a baseball fan who tries in vain to convince the new Queens-based team [the soon-to-be Mets] to adopt a pro-labor song as its anthem. But Lenny never finds a place where his efforts as a provocateur are welcome. Forbes, on the other hand, is fortifying a place where his are essential.

* * *

Jodorowsky's Dune is a documentary about director Alejandro Jodorowsky's quest to make a film adaptation of the Frank Herbert science fiction novel. The project never made it off the launch pad but in the mid-'70s Jodorowsky and his collaborators spent months recruiting cast members, including Salvador Dalí, Orson Welles, and Mick Jagger. They also drafted a shot-by-shot breakdown of the proposed movie. "Fever dream" might be more apt—the book was comprised of three thousand illustrations and the film-to-be had a running time of fourteen hours.

* * *

Explaining the band's name, Hwang says, "Sing is a common sound in the Chinese language. Depending upon the tone, inflection, context, and dialect, the meanings and the calligraphy vary greatly. I hear Sing as a sound."

"So in that sense it's like a syllable," I ask, "a building block, a part of a larger whole?"

"Yes," Hwang replies, "I should ask a linguist as to what sonic unit this sound would be categorized."

* * *

As with any book-to-film adaptation, Jodorowsky wanted to make changes to the source material. Among them was an alternate ending in which Duke Leto's son Paul was killed. Paul's consciousness spread among the masses and sparked a rebirth of the planet. Dune was transformed from a desert to a garden, vast and verdant. From one can come many.

* * *

Hwang leans into the beat as he counts off. There are plans afoot. *Follow me*. His fingers slide along the strings, inward, toward him, evoking the highest, faintest, most fragile of pitches, the smallest specks of paint that prompt a closer look at the canvas. I've been so focused on Hwang's role as composer and conductor that I'd momentarily lost sight of the performer.

Then there's an explosion. The band in full force. They're in one place physically but sonically scattered, like a Sol LeWitt wall drawing, so many lines radiating, yet carefully placed within the larger piece.

* * *

Jason Kao Hwang: "The music is a house, with the score's quintessential melodies, rhythms, harmonies, and textures offering rooms in which musicians extemporaneously sing. In this dramatic architecture, the unique voice of each musician is empowered to individually interpret and also transcend interpretation to become an originating spirit that is inextricably unified to the composition's destiny. This is how music grows greater than the imagination of one to become a meta-language of memories, dreams, and hope. This is how my compositions house imagination, identity, and greater purpose. This is the jazz of Sing House."

Ben Monder | Michael Bogdanffy-Kriegh

The Infinite on a Smaller Scale
Ben Monder

"If I walk quiet / I hear the bird's pretty tune
High in the hills / Me and this beautiful moon"
—Kim Deal, "Beautiful Moon"

Winter hates jazz. That's the latest joke among the Quinn's faithful. Last week's show was cancelled due to snow. The previous week's, too. Until a couple of hours ago tonight was headed for the same fate. School closed early and I spent the afternoon shoveling the driveway and raking the roof. There was so much ice clinging to our front porch that I had to resort to using a hammer, kneeling and bashing.

* * *

Ben Monder could not be more gentle as he coaxes sounds from his guitar. His left hand cruises the fretboard while his right hand hovers above the pick-ups. The notes fly like sparks, spectacular oranges and reds. He has a speed skater's deceptive effort-to-movement ratio, gliding great lengths on easy pushes.

Monder is seated, one foot on the floor, the other casually propped on a monitor. He's wearing a winter hat and unassuming pants and shirt. He resembles Fugazi's Ian MacKaye. He looks like Emil, our plumber, too. It's like the old *Electric Company* segment—"It's the plumber! I've come to fix the sink!"—but refitted: "I'm the guitarist. I've come to ease your pain." That could be taken philosophically, but right now, after all the shoveling and raking and hacking, Monder's playing brings on pure physical relief.

* * *

There was solace in hearing the roar of my neighbor's snow blower, chomping through the accumulation covering our shared driveway. But the beast of a machine kept jamming up. Keith had to stop every few feet, lift the handles, and slam down the front to unclog the auger. When we finished I asked if he wanted to go to Quinn's. I was ready to toss in a sales pitch, remind him of the last time we'd gone, but he didn't even ask who was playing, just wanted to know when we should leave.

* * *

The opening scenes of Debra Granik's *Winter's Bone* say so much, thanks in large part to the dearth of dialogue. In those first minutes Ree Dolly (Jennifer Lawrence) moves through her world showing how she is surrounded by others, supportive of and supported by them, but very much on a solitary journey.

* * *

James sees Keith and me looking for a table and invites us to join him. It's his birthday. Well-wishers stop by. They text, too, his phone lighting up every few seconds. He's amped. He's been talking about this show for weeks. "You *have* to see this one. Have to." Something about best or favorite or most important modern guitarist. I forget the phrasing but

I've come to trust him. Hard to fathom that all of this—the place, the people, the performances—was new to me a year ago.

Quinn's is closing soon temporarily, shutting down for a couple of weeks for renovations. It was a good time to take stock and begin shaping the book. I wasn't planning to write about tonight's show but James's enthusiasm won me over, so here I am, notebook in hand, transfixed by the sight of Monder's fingers spider crawling back and forth. The guitar neck is so small in his grasp, so seemingly easy to navigate.

* * *

Of all Jackie Chan's stunts, the one that comes to mind most often is probably the simplest. He's running down an alley, desperate to escape, as always. The wall to his left is too high to scale. He runs at the wall, leaps, uses his left foot to push toward the opposite wall, which he then uses to propel himself over the first wall. Frightened, fleeing human turned vertical pinball. It's probably the safest of his stunts, but it's a brilliant display of will and ability. Unlike his other stunts, this one— even just the memory of it—leaves me with the momentary impression that I too could scale walls. Even when rational thought returns, I'm left with the comforting sense that one of us is capable of such feats.

* * *

Keith and I go back and forth as Monder plays on.

"It's like two guitars."

"It's like two guitars and a bass—do you hear *that*?"

"Yes. Two guitars and bass, *and* a viola, too."

We're watching the same show. Arguably we're hearing the same sounds.

But neither of us has a scorecard that matches up with the sonics; we're coming up short in establishing any sort of one-to-one correspondence. It's like watching close magic—*I'm just a few feet away. I can see everything. I can explain none of it.*

Monder's motivations are different obviously; he's not out to be coy or deceptive. Yet still we search and poke and prod, look for tricks or codes; try to make sense of something so far beyond our reach, humanize it. All the while marveling more than minimizing.

"Did you see that double jointed pinky move?"

"Those are finger extensions, right?"

"How can one person *do* that?"

* * *

My mom went in for surgery last week. My brother Casey sent out progress reports throughout the day. I was at lunch when she came out of surgery. I was halfway to Syracuse by the time she was awake and alert enough to manage a bowl of soup. All signs were, and continue to be, positive.

* * *

"It's not really jazz, is it?"

"No."

"Free jazz?"

"I don't think so."

"But it's not rock…"

"No."

"Or classical."

"No."

"But it's kind of all of them."

"Yes."

* * *

Ree's most viable option is to sell off the one asset at her disposal: the trees on her family's property. But she's too proud, too defiant, duty bound to do right, knowing that this will take her down the path of greatest resistance.

* * *

Monder has a streak of that. With his talent he could easily raise his profile with celebrity studio work, coast down more lucrative roads, lean into the flash and glitz. But he doesn't and there's something admirable, noble in his choices. I don't want to reduce Monder to caricature, liken him to a monk laboring in isolation.[6] He may talk less than Ree Dolly but his wit comes through when he does.

Ben Monder: [Addressing the audience, but without a mic]

Keepnews: "We can get you a mic."

---

6 Monder subsequently appeared on David Bowie's final studio album, *Blackstar*.

Monder: [Speaking into newly acquired mic] "Sounds the same to me but I guess I'm being amplified somewhere. [To the sound person] Can you cut the hi-mids? I'm kidding. That last song was 'Window Panes.' It was written for younger arms."

* * *

As we discuss her recovery, my mom mentions getting together with friends from her community theater days. This bodes well. She also talks about the challenges she's facing, among them the difficulty of grasping small objects. I ask about the utensil grips she used in the hospital and recall our pre-surgery talks, her reluctance to ask for help, both admirable and stubborn.

"Have you asked about those grips?"

"Well…"

Forward in some ways, circling in others.

* * *

Both of Monder's feet find their way to the floor for the final tune, foreshadowing a different turn. The flourishes are more demonstrative as the volume and speed and distortion ramp up to monumental masses of sound, colors streaking by, distorting space and time, like the final stages of David Bowman's journey in *2001: A Space Odyssey.*

James Keepnews, perhaps emboldened by the confluence of such an ending to such a show on such a night, makes an on-mic request for an encore.

Keepnews: [To audience] "Two words: jazz, motherfucker! [To Monder] I've heard you do it with a trio. How about solo—'Wichita Lineman'?"

Monder: I'll try it. Really might not work. I don't know.

Keith leans over and asks if I want to stay for one more.

Joe Morris | Michael Bogdanffy-Kriegh

It's Not About Time
The Spanish Donkey

"Take the hands off the clock
We're going to be here a while"
—Camper Van Beethoven, "Eye of Fatima"

It's chilly tonight, cold in ways our backyard thermometer can't measure, cold in ways that slow down everything and induce a huddle-round-the-fire feeling, triggers the need to pull closer.

The Spanish Donkey push forth enormous arrays of sound—guitar and keyboards mixing and melting, drums securing the perimeter. Maybe defining the perimeter is more apt. The band's outer edge is more permeable membrane than rigidly defined border—it has to be with the frequency of ideas flowing in and out and their ever-shifting dimensions. Keyboardist Jamie Saft pounds on quarter notes. Drummer Mike Pride streams steady eighths, and guitarist Joe Morris, well, I can't pinpoint what he's up to. Yet for all the different dynamics, there's something highly concentrated, all the parts pulling in more than pushing away, more centripetal than centrifugal.

The band's name has me thinking of *Don Quixote*, specifically Sancho Panza, the realist, the voice of practicality.

Joe Morris looks down at his gear. He maneuvers massive sounds, yet he's reserved in his responses, stoic, the cool-headed engineer at mission control. I notice the organ, rich and vibrant. Did Jamie Saft just start that or has he been locked into it for the past five minutes? I drift to the drums. Pride fluctuates, avoids easily defined beats. Before long Morris reenters, like storm clouds you've seen coming for miles but still manage to startle when they open up. When I stick with one player I lose track of the others, never sure for how long, then I'm surprised by what's developed elsewhere.

* * *

Season two of *House of Cards* opens on a long shot of a D.C. park at night. There's no one in sight and it's very quiet, too quiet for a city park. You scan the frame for people, evidence of action. Eventually two figures appear. They're dressed in black and jogging side by side. Initially they're too distant to distinguish. As they slowly emerge from the dark you realize it's Frank and Claire Underwood. The continuous action lets you choose where your attention goes. You're given the whole and with it a chance to sift through the parts.

* * *

Last weekend I went to a reading in Brooklyn. I ran into my friend Brendan at Grand Central. We walked a couple blocks west to catch the F train. Before we got on the subway he was saying that he should have driven. We talked on the train but couldn't lose track of time because neither of us was familiar with the F line. We had to keep looking at the map, checking the stops, and trying to decode the garbled announcements. When we got to Brooklyn we saw ample parking and little traffic. Brendan was convinced he'd made the wrong decision. "I should have driven."

* * *

The Spanish Donkey can blister, play loud, push the amplitudes. But for all the band's volume, its relative restraint is even more noteworthy. It's not about the horizontal (movement or structure) or the vertical (changes in pitch or tone). It's this sense of branching out yet staying within close proximity.

* * *

Between sets I order a drink. The bartender, George, chats with Joe Morris. George takes a moment to break away to take my order. He apologizes but there's no need. While holding court, Morris uses the phrase "static density." I can't define it but it's apropos for the Spanish Donkey.

* * *

Back on stage Morris shoots through the stratosphere. Meso- and thermospheres, too. He heads for the exosphere, still somewhat bound by gravity but merging with other realms. Other guitarists may reach these levels, but during a solo, an aberration, a break from the routine. For Morris, it's the norm, cruising altitude.

* * *

Later, still unsure of how to explain static density, I email Morris and he responds, "The forward motion of time as pulse is so slow that it feels like it's barely moving. Therefore we can make form without being burdened by the pulse, unless we chose to be."

* * *

The reading was outdoors, on the Hamilton's sidewalk in Windsor Terrace. The afternoon was roll-up-the-sleeves warm, a perfect day to listen to our friend Brian read from his new book and watch tattooed helicopter parents stroll by with canvas bags of co-op veggies, trailed by scooter kids in soccer jerseys. After the reading we went inside to have dinner. The food was good and the laughter loud. We forgot the time and stayed late. Brendan said he was glad he took the train.

* * *

Jamie Saft—army jacket clad, belly length beard and short cropped hair (anti-mullet?)—radiates holiday cheer. Or crush-the-state radicalism. Maybe both. He holds down the middle, imparts stability, links the band like Yggdrasil, the tree that links the nine worlds of Norse mythology. Without him it falls apart.

* * *

In Chris Offutt's "Sawdust," the narrator, Junior, living in the hills of Kentucky, wrestles with the contradictions between his family's values and those of the outside world. He thinks about getting his GED and, among other things, he's confused by math: "a pile of stove wood doesn't equal a tree. It made me wonder where the sawdust went to in a math problem."

* * *

Pride sets a gong on top of his floor tom and sheets of mallet on metal ring out. Then he drops the mallet and appears to pull a stick from behind his back, Green Arrow-style. (Where's the boxing glove stick?)

* * *

In the coming months, Morris and Saft will collaborate on records with the likes of Joe McPhee, Mary Halvorson, and Wadada Leo Smith. Pride is equally versatile, including a stint with punk legends MDC.

While touring with MDC, Pride encountered Lemmy from Motörhead backstage at a festival. "Lemmy said, 'I heard you play jazz.' But I'm not sure it was a compliment with him." Pride also met Rob Halford from Judas Priest. "After we played he said, 'You play jazz, don't you? I was listening, mate!'"

As a trio they stir up different densities, rotating through high, medium, and low, which generate movement, push things along. I mention this to Michael Bogdanffy-Kriegh. He says it reminds him of a quote from *Moby Dick*, "the tornadoed Atlantic of my being."

I'm fascinated with *Moby Dick* but comprehend little of it. Within days the context of the line has evaporated beyond the sense of Ishmael finding himself in a birthing center, which might be construed as the center of the universe. I mention this in an email exchange with my friend Sean, who clarifies and closes with this:

"In the midst of all this chaos, the whaling boat is suddenly stuck inside a beautiful, serene, peaceful place where humans almost never tread."

There's something about the Spanish Donkey that elicits the timeless, the epic, the classic. Maybe it's the way they treat time, shove it aside, and take us places rarely seen.

* * *

Offut's Junior, a modern Sancho Panza of sorts, adds, "After all that ciphering, there wasn't anything to show for the work, nothing to clean up, nothing to look at." It sounds like a description of most commercial music—linear, sequential, everything accounted for, no mess and easy to digest.

* * *

Joe Morris: "I use the term free music. Free from any industry, institutional, or critical oversight."

* * *

The Minutemen followed their greatest success, *Double Nickels on the Dime*, with the *Project: Mersh* EP. "Mersh" being Minutemen speak for "commercial." The cover art shows a trio of executives gathered in a boardroom. Behind them a line graph. In the foreground one exec cries out, "I got it! We'll have them write hit songs."

* * *

Joe Morris: "People ask, 'Do you make any money? Will it be historically significant? My answer is, 'Screw you.' It took me a long time to get to that."

* * *

Nights at Quinn's are all about the sawdust, not the mess itself, but all that goes into making the mess, insuring that there is something to show for the work. I flash back to Werner Herzog's *The Wheel of Time*. Gathering for an initiation ceremony, a group of monks builds a sand mandala, a large, intricately detailed sand sculpture the size of a ping pong table. Hunched over the table wearing masks and holding narrow metal funnels, they toil for days, laboring in eighteen-hour shifts. No attempt is made to preserve the mandala when the ceremony ends. The monks' work is swept aside like sawdust.

* * *

The next day there's an online dialogue about the show. Joe Morris writes, "It's places like [Quinn's] that are the hope and the future of all of this. Small, local, and brave as hell is always the best."

Steve Ventura | Michael Bogdanffy-Kriegh

EPILOGUE

In the foreword to *Sugar Among the Freaks*, writer Lewis Nordan describes struggling with a troublesome story. He takes out his "miserable legal pad and its failed fiction," rereads the story, and circles in red anything that catches his attention, "each image, detail, idea, turn of phrase" that is worth saving. I associate red ink with corrections, a way of identifying miscues and errors, finding what's flawed. Nordan flips that, uses red circles to signify what's right, what carries him forward.

The place at 330 Main Street in Beacon has been the site of countless nourishing performances and experiences, a stream of red circles. Still, I want to think that it's more than those musical moments, individually or en masse.

* * *

Like everyone else, I have friends and coworkers with whom I disagreed about the 2016 presidential election. But when the subject came up at get togethers or at work, the conversations centered around civics and civility; the importance of the former, the lack of the latter. Meanwhile in class, conversations focused on listening, discussing differences, and understanding the process of an election. I was spared direct exposure to the extreme positions that I glimpsed in the media. Until a week before the election.

One night, waiting to meet my wife at a local brew pub, I was listening to the bartender, Dan, speak glowingly about a recent Morrissey concert he'd seen in New York. Dan has a vast knowledge of all things hoppy and malted. I've come to trust his recommendations. Naively, I assumed that this, combined with his taste in music, would extend to politics. When he said that he couldn't wait for the campaign to be over, I felt a sympathetic rant surfacing.

I had no way of knowing that the conversation was about to lurch into the sub-tabloid. Before I knew it Dan, the same Dan who'd regaled me with tales of Morrissey working his melancholy magic and tipped me off to the best Belgian ales, was pointing to a "very reliable website" on his phone and telling everyone within earshot that Hillary and Bill Clinton were practicing Satanists.

* * *

A few months ago, my son and I went to see Joe McPhee and Michael Bisio perform on a Sunday afternoon in New Paltz. They were taken by the sight of Sean, eight years old, scooting around snapping pictures. When another Sunday afternoon show came along, shortly after the election, Sean eagerly asked to go.

Bisio and his wife Dawn hosted an after party. Sean was in such a good mood, so eager to impress, that he voluntarily filled his plate with more carrot sticks than cookies. After returning with a second plate of snacks, I asked him about the music. He'd enjoyed it but was more interested in Joe McPhee's "Black Lives Matter" button. "That's pretty cool," he said. He was sharing his thoughts more than asking for mine, there with me but thinking on his own. I encouraged him to share this with Joe.

Sean walked across the room and tapped Joe on the elbow. I couldn't hear their exchange above the talk and the music but could see Joe lean over to listen.

As we walked to the car, I asked Sean what he'd said.

"I told him I liked his button and that he should keep wearing it."

* * *

In the midst of Dan's diatribe, another customer sat to my left. He didn't speak up until Dan stepped away.

"I can't wait for it to be over." His tone was weary. I assumed that he was reacting to Dan. I assumed that I had an ally. He continued before I could attempt to connect.

"Things are only going to get worse. Obama isn't going to leave office, you know." He claimed that the president would refuse to relinquish the presidency and remain in power for two additional years. He'd learned of the pending coup from an off duty FBI agent after working out at the gym. The distance I'd been feeling increased exponentially. It was alienating. I felt like a stranger in a familiar land.

* * *

I emailed Joe, thanking him for the show and for the questions Sean started to ask about Black Lives Matter and race and fairness. Joe wrote,

"Sean is my hero. Thanks to young people like him, I have hope in this dark hour." He also asked to send Sean a gift.

* * *

A few days later, the package from Joe arrived containing, among other things, a letter:

> Hello Sean,
>
> Thanks so much for coming out to our concerts. I know when you are in the house the music will be good.
>
> I wear a Black Lives Matter badge like Batman's bat symbol or Superman's "S" as a reminder that we live at a time that unfortunately we need this constant reminder. The fact is, all life matters and perhaps the time will come when Black Lives Matter will no longer be needed as a symbol. Respect for all life will be in our hearts and minds.
>
> I would love to hear you playing in a band one day or better, vote for you when you run for president of the United States.
>
> All the best and a Merry Christmas and Happy New Year,
>
> Your friend,
> Joe McPhee

* * *

Joe often pays tribute to living artists, naming songs for musicians who have inspired him. 1992's *Impressions of Jimmy Giuffre* contains a song titled "Give Them Their Flowers While They're Here."

* * *

Among the gifts was a copy of *Candy*, a set of live recordings with Joe and Norwegian drummer Paal Nilssen-Love. In the liner notes, Nilssen-Love talks about what a privilege it is listening to McPhee's *Nation Time*, how it spurs him on, turns things back on the listener, as in: "Okay, what are YOU going to do?"

In hindsight, *The Other Night at Quinn's* is an attempt to do my part, respond to that challenge, celebrate red circle moments, and pass along well-deserved flowers.

Brendan O'Mara and Melissa DeLorenzo at the counter | Michael Bogdanffy-Kriegh

Patron at booth | Michael Bogdanffy-Kriegh

MONDAY NIGHT JAZZ SESSIONS @ THE NEW

Incomparable jazz artists from the Hudson Valley, NYC and worldwide converge each Monday night starting in October at Beacon's hottest new live music venue, QUINN'S • NO COVER CHARGE!

OCTOBER 7th • WILLIAM PARKER
The legendary bassist and bandleader launches this series with a special solo, multi-instrumental performance

OCTOBER 14th • CHRIS KELSEY
Local saxophonist & writer Kelsey and his band What I Say celebrate their new CD release The Electric Miles Project

OCTOBER 21st • TANI TABBAL
The accomplished Hudson Valley-based drummer throws down in a duo with saxophonist Ben Newsome

OCTOBER 28th • NIX/GRILLIOT
Celebrated guitarist in Ornette Coleman's original Prime Time band Bern Nix performs with virtuoso bassist François Grilliot

8 PM EVERY MONDAY • FREE ADMISSION
330 Main St, Beacon, NY • quinnsbeacon.com
(coming in November: Karl Berger, Ted Daniel & more!)

First Quinn's flyer | James Keepnews

All the Quiet Sounds

Andrew Drury & Mike Faloon

Michael Bogdanffy-Kriegh

THANKS

Dave Berger, Karl Berger, Sarah Bernstein, Jonas Bers, Katy Binder, Keith Binder, Michael Bisio, Holly Bogdanffy, Jaimie Branch, Mike Burdge, Juan Pablo Carletti, Damian Cleary, John Colpitts, Chris Corsano, Melissa DiLorenzo, Mike Dopazo, Welf Dorr, Yvonne Drazan, Avram Fefer, Joe Fiedler, Casey Faloon, Pat Faloon, Steve Faloon, Ken Filiano, Christopher Forbes, Michael Galvin, Mike Gamble, Allison Glassman, Juice Glover, Rebecca Griffin, Jason Kao Hwang, Chris Kelsey, Thomas King, Kirk Knuffke, Vince Kueter, Daniel Levin, Dan Loomis, Matt Luczak, Alice Marsh-Elmer, Ravish Momin, Cooper-Moore, Joe Morris, Lisa Panepinto, Sam Pluta, Mike Pride, Dan Rigney, Jay Rosen, Josh Rutner, Jamie Saft, Ingrid Sertso, Tom Schmitz, Yukie Schmitz, Shawn Sizemore, Ches Smith, Matthew Specktor, Iola Taylor, Mike White, Michael Wimberly, Jennifer Federico, and Jim Ruland.

Additional gratitude to the musicians who stormed through Quinn's but are not included in these pages. They merit a book of their own.

Michael Bogdanffy-Kriegh

ACKNOWLEDGMENTS

When I first walked into Quinn's, I was thinking about what I'd hear and didn't consider who I'd meet. The first people to reach out, to ask about the open notebook on the countertop, were James Keepnews and Steve Ventura. I'd be forever grateful had they "only" booked the dozens of shows I saw at Quinn's. They were supportive from the outset, sharing a wealth of knowledge and boundless enthusiasm, always treating me like a peer and friend.

Joe McPhee is the hypocenter of this book, the point of origin. He's the reason I first came to Quinn's. It's ironic his *Nation Time* album was my entry into his vast discography because the numerous shows I've seen subsequently have sounded nothing like that record. He's a boundless talent and uncommonly humble. I hope this book conveys some measure of the gratitude I feel for the ways in which his music and outlook have shaped my life.

Meeting another person compelled to document the performances at Quinn's was a relief. The first columns I posted online were well received but lacking. They were virtually all text with no original photography, which diminished the sense of place. Thankfully, Michael Bogdanffy-Kreigh allowed me to include his photographs with subsequent posts. I can't imagine this book without his contributions.

For their ongoing feedback, editorial and otherwise, I'm indebted to Brian Cogan, Brett Essler, and Brendan Kiernan, especially in the year leading up to publication. They combed through each chapter and helped shape the book. They went above and beyond by writing a blurb (Brian), producing a promotional video (Brett), and providing a final copy edit (Brendan). They spur me on as friends and writers. This book never would have crossed the finish line without them.

The people at Quinn's—staff and patrons—have always made me feel comfortable. No easy task for an introvert at a bar. The wobbly countertop was home to countless conversations before and after shows, sometimes during, too. Thanks to Craig Nixon, Mark Pisanelli, Eric Porter, George Spafford, and others for engaging and indulging.

This project provided excuses to reach out to a wide range of talented people. I'm grateful to Hallie Bulliet, John Ross Bowie, Sean Carswell, Erica Dicker, Chris Gethard, Mary Halvorson, Ingrid Laubrock, Nørb Rozek, David Shields, Steve Swell, and Jason Turbow for sharing their thoughts on various aspects of the creative process.

I hoped to entice one or two distinguished voices to write blurbs. I had no idea the likes of Kevin Dunn, Wayne Kramer, Mike Watt, Jennifer Whiteford, Josh Wilker, *and* Rudy Wurlitzer would read and respond to the manuscript. I can think of no better way to top off the celebration that is *The Other Night at Quinn's*.

Seeing pieces from this collection in print along the way helped on many levels. Thanks to Andrew Drury for collaborating on a one-shot zine, *All the Quiet Sounds*, and Tobias Carroll at *Vol. 1 Brooklyn* for posting a chapter. Likewise to my frequent tourmate Michael Fournier at *Cabildo Quarterly*, who rounded out a Triple Crown by also reading early drafts and writing a blurb.

About halfway through the process of assembling the parts into a whole, I became interested in the history of Beacon. I couldn't properly prune what I'd found and almost got lost down the rabbit hole. Fortunately, I met Bev Turcy and Bob Murphy. While working for the city, Bev guided me through the history of 330 Main St. She and her husband and sister,

Joe Turcy and Betty Ann Coughlin, later shared their recollections of growing up in Beacon. I met Bob Murphy at the Beacon Historical Society and he led me to the archival photographs included here. Their stories and images provided much-needed historical context.

The book's interviews would have languished untranscribed far too long were it not for Madeline Bridenbaugh and Matthew Hart. They were so thorough, quick, and patient. Thanks for bearing with me as I learned, however slowly, about mic placement.

Editorial insights and excessive "that" removal thanks to Kari Hamanaka. She knows the rules and has a great sense of when to bend, when to break, and when to adhere. Among other things, she contributed greatly to solving the Mystery of the Missing Apostrophes. I rest easier once Kari's sifted through things.

Lifeboat thanks to Todd Taylor. The book was in danger of sinking before he entered the picture. He's punk rock through and through, and I didn't expect him to take interest in a book rooted in free jazz and improvised music. He picked up on the bigger ideas in this "jazz book that's not really about jazz," about the vitality and importance of non-commercial music and the appeal of another thriving underground scene. Few people balance the big picture with such an eye for detail and fewer still opt to collaborate.

If you're lucky, you draw the best of your parents' traits and at some point develop a deeper appreciation for them as people. There are too many things to cite here but for starters, Mom, thanks for your quiet perseverance and, Dad, thanks for sharing your appreciation for music. I love you and don't say it often enough.

Finally, deep love and admiration for Maggie and Sean for growing up with big hearts and open minds.

RECOMMENDED LISTENING AND PLAYLIST

Dozens of musicians appear in *The Other Night at Quinn's* and they have released hundreds of records. I've barely scratched the surface but these are among my favorites so far.

–Mike

Sarah Bernstein Quartet—*Still/Free* (Leo)
Michael Bisio—*Accortet* (Relative Pitch)
Jaimie Branch—*Fly or Die* (International Anthem)
Andrew Drury—*Content Provider* (Soup & Sound)
Avram Fefer—*Ritual* (Clean Feed)
Alan Juice Glover—*Kings of Infinite Space* (Omolade)
Mary Halvorson—*Meltframe* (Firehouse)
Mary Halvorson Octet—*Away with You* (Firehouse)
Jason Kao Hwang—*Sing House* (Euonymus)
Kirk Knuffke—*Arms & Hands* (Royal Potato Family)
Ingrid Laubrock's Anti-House—*Roulette of the Cradle* (Intakt)
Daniel Levin—*Organic Modernism* (Clean Feed)
Joe McPhee—*Nation Time* (CjR)
Joe McPhee & Chris Corsano—*Under a Double Moon* (Roaratorio)
Man Forever with So Percussion—*Ryonen* (Thrill Jockey)
Steve Swell Quintet—*Soul Travelers* (Rogue Art)

I also compiled a free playlist of many of the musicians mentioned in this book. Give it a listen:
gorskypress.bandcamp.com/album/the-other-night-at-quinns-playlist

RAZORCAKE/GORSKY PRESS

Razorcake/Gorsky Press, Inc. is a 501(c)(3) non-profit organization based out of Los Angeles, Calif. We publish both books and zines.

Gorsky Press was founded in 1999 and has published twenty-two books. Our books run the gamut from poetry, novels, short story collections, zine collections, and comics.

Razorcake was founded in 2001. *Razorcake*, our bi-monthly zine, provides consistent coverage of do-it-yourself punk culture that you won't find anywhere else. We believe in positive, progressive, community-friendly DIY punk.

We do our part.

Visit our websites for updates and information.

www.gorskypress.com
www.razorcake.org

MICHAEL BOGDANFFY-KRIEGH

Michael Bogdanffy-Kriegh is a self-trained fine art photographer who lives in Beacon, N.Y. Formally trained as an architect, he made the decision to focus exclusively on photography in 2013.

Michael has developed his fine art photography through a daily meditative walking practice during which he photographs whatever compels him.

His music photography work focuses on jazz, folk, blues, and rock bands playing at local venues.

His work has appeared in numerous exhibitions, including *Flora*, a group show at Davis Orton Gallery in Hudson, N.Y.; *Welcome: Page by Page*, an exhibit of artist books curated by Hannah Frieser at the Center for Photography in Woodstock; and the *21st Annual Juried Show: Peter Urban Legacy Exhibition*, juried by Jim Casper, at the Griffin Museum of Photography in Winchester, Mass.

Michael's photographs have also been published in *Shots Magazine* issue #129 and issue #130, the annual portfolio edition.

Michael lives with his wife Holly, along with their dogs Chas and Augie and cat Ziggy.

MIKE FALOON

Mike Faloon is a former DJ, dishwasher, and drummer. He is the author of *The Hanging Gardens of Split Rock* and co-editor of *Fan Interference*. Faloon co-founded *Go Metric* and *Zisk* zines and has contributed to *Cabildo Quarterly*, *Cashiers du Cinemart*, *Razorcake*, *Submerging Writers*, and *Vol. 1 Brooklyn*. He has toured often in the past decade, with stops at the UCB Theatre and the Baseball Hall of Fame. Faloon currently lives in upstate New York.